SHINE!
Inspirational Stories of Choosing Success Over Adversity

Volume III

Prominence Publishing

Book and Cover design by Prominence Publishing.
www.prominencepublishing.com

SHINE/Multiple Authors -- 1st ed.

ISBN: 978-1-988925-33-2

Table of Contents

Introduction 1

What Do You Like? 7

About the Author Shelley Hewins Brown........................ 18

Two Wheels to Four: Flipping and Forgiving 21

About the Author Julie Sawchuk...................................... 52

The Importance of Self Belief.. 55

About the Author Rosalind Ferry 71

Six Months to Give 73

About the Author Robin Levesque 92

And the Journey Continues 95

About the Author Yanira Cuellar 107

Using the Power of Positive Thought 109

About the Author Beth Oldfield...................................... 124

Source Energy 127

About the Author Dr. Lesya Anna 144

Losing and Gaining Control... 147

About the Author Izabela Adams.................................... 163

Strategies For Overcoming Anxiety................................ 167

About the Author Trish Scoular....................................... 187

Introduction

Having worked with more than 700 authors in the last eight years, I have seen a good number of stories about overcoming adversity. No matter who tells the story, or how the story is told, they always leave me feeling inspired and encouraged to overcome any challenges that I may encounter.

We are all stronger than we think we are. You are stronger than you think you are. You can do anything you set your mind to!

I am thrilled to be publishing volume three of the SHINE! book series. I hope that these authors' stories inspire and encourage you, too. Please know that no matter what is happening in your life, no matter what challenges you are facing, there is <u>always a way</u>.

You CAN overcome anything that life throws at you!

It wasn't that many years ago that I was facing my own intense adversity. Prior to 2009, I had a successful marketing agency with clients all over North America. Our gross revenue was half a million dollars a year, and we had a lifestyle to match. I had no idea that my business was going to fail... But that is exactly what happened.

I had a sales person working for me that I dearly loved. I would have given him anything. In fact, I always joked that he was my 'brother from another mother'. I helped him when he needed it; I encouraged him and trained him to be a highly successful high-income earning sales person. I compensated him with a 50% commission rate, which was very generous. I spent $7,000 a month on leads so that he could concentrate on sales instead of prospecting.

One day, he abruptly left my company and took all our top clients with him. It was a massive betrayal. This also happened to be at the exact time that the economy was crashing. As a result of these two factors, our revenue decreased from half million dollars a year to about $40,000 a year, seemingly overnight. There was nothing I could do about it because although I owned the company and technically those clients were mine, they didn't know me, and they were following him out of loyalty. Even if I took the matter to court, and even if I won, I had lost those clients and I could never get them back. Of course, I was also angry at myself for letting this happen.

Inside my head, I felt like a complete failure. And I was so deeply ashamed; I did not want anyone to know what was happening. At a time when I should have been reaching out to friends and family for support, I hid. And I cried. A lot.

I could not sleep. I could not work. I felt completely alone. I was going out of my mind trying to figure out what to do to save my company. Nothing I had done in the past was working now. Marketing tactics that used to work were not working because no one was buying.

My self-talk was incredibly negative.

You're a loser.

You're so stupid.

You will never amount to anything.

You are not good enough.

You're a complete failure.

You don't deserve anything good.

My negative self-talk was so pervasive that I also started to think that I was ugly, fat, and not lovable. I remember looking in the mirror sometimes and thinking, *You're so disgusting.* This is how I would talk to myself!

Looking back on it now from a place of peace and contentment, I am shocked that this is how my thought processes were. But it's true.

Please understand: Your brain will believe anything you think. It's your command centre. If you think, "I can't do anything right," your brain will take that as a command and make that true for you.

If you think, "I am always late," your brain will make sure that you are always late.

As soon as I flipped my thinking from negative to positive, everything started to get better. It takes time, but it works.

To be honest, it took me about three years to get over that betrayal. I spent so many hours feeling angry and sad. I replayed events over and over in my mind. I had entire imaginary conversations in my head, repeatedly! (Have you done this, too?)

Because I was the sole provider for my family, I quickly had to change gears and figure out a way to support my three children. It was then that I decided to write my first book. I was so afraid that it was going to fail, that I wrote it under a fake name so that nobody would know it was me. (True story!) The funny thing is, I still had my marketing skills and I managed to make the book a #1 best seller on Amazon. Imagine my shock! I started thinking, Maybe I'm not a complete loser after all? Maybe I'm not a total failure? Maybe writing books is the answer? To support my family, I wrote six more books that year, and it was tough, I'm not going to sugarcoat it. Keep in mind that I had three young children between the ages of four and nine. I could only write from 10 o'clock at night until midnight, but I did it almost every single night for one year. Yes, I was exhausted.

Does that sound fun? It was not. This is a lesson that I share with my clients and my students in my writing and publishing programs: **Sometimes you have to do what you don't want to do, to have what you want to have.**

When people ask me if I'm a writer, I reply, "No, but I'm an author," and there's a difference, believe me.

A wise woman named Sandra Yancey (The CEO of the eWomen Network) once said to me, "Betrayals don't happen TO you, they happen FOR you." When I heard that, it was a turning point in my life. I felt a complete sense of calm come over me and I realized that I had been spending way too much energy on feeling angry instead of forgiving and taking responsibility for it. When something bad happens, it may not be your fault, but it is your responsibility. I started to feel really grateful, too. If that betrayal hadn't happened for me, I would not be where I am today. I would not have had the chance to work with so many amazing, inspiring people who are all making the world a better place. Can you imagine how grateful I am to play even a tiny part in that? When I can help someone realize their dream of becoming a published author, it brings me intense joy. When they get to hold their book in their hands for the very first time, I feel so emotional for them because I remember that feeling and I know how overwhelming it is. It feels like the first time for me over and over again. It really is the greatest feeling in the world!

I hope the following stories inspire and encourage you. Always remember that whatever you are going through, it is not the end – keep going.

Wishing you all the best,
Suzanne Doyle-Ingram
CEO, Prominence Publishing
Creator of The Expert Author Program

CHAPTER ONE

What Do You Like?

By Shelley Hewins Brown

I had never thought about this question in quite the same way before that special day.

It was late in the afternoon on a dreary and cold October day. Dusk had already set in and with the overcast skies, the darkness made it almost feel like night. It was the Canadian Thanksgiving weekend; it felt weird to be out walking with my daughter looking for something to fill our minds. Usually we would be home planning a big family dinner. But, not this year. There we were, strolling down a trendy little street in Winnipeg, Manitoba on what felt like a sad and dreary, grey day.

We sauntered slowly, arm in arm, not really talking to one another and sipping on our pumpkin spice lattes. It had only been a couple of weeks since her Dad and I had separated, and we were both feeling sad and dreary too. As we walked quietly, noses tucked into our heavy coats to stay warm, we happened upon a little antique store. We both wandered in. It wasn't something that she or I had ever really done before. We didn't collect or even admire antiques, but somehow, we ended up inside Selim's Antique Store.

It was warm in there and once inside, we stood for a moment at the entrance just navigating which path to take. It wasn't what you would expect in a store of old things. There was no "old" smell and it was absolutely meticulous no matter which direction you looked. It wasn't a bunch of dust covered, discarded things at all; it seemed to be filled with what was more like treasures.

As we stood there, a sharp dressed, elderly man came over to greet us. He had a gentle smile that covered his aged skin and you could hear his smile in his words. He was so finely dressed in a dark suit, white shirt and blue tie. He had shiny silver hair that was neatly styled, and his fashionable glasses sat atop his perfectly straight nose. Not a big man in stature, but his presence in the store was imposing. You could sense he loved it and wanted you to as well. It showed in how he dressed for work, especially on a holiday Sunday when many stores were closed. His joy was exemplified in that big smile. He welcomed us to the store and encouraged us to take our time and have a look around. So, we did.

It took both Kenzie and I several minutes to move slowly through the aisles of the small space, looking at the many beautifully displayed items. Eventually we spoke to one another, commenting on how tidy and organized the amazing little place was. We ended up standing in what felt like the center of the store. In front of us was this overwhelmingly large, dark brown china cabinet that was full of all kinds of things. Each item was neatly placed with just the right amount of space between them. There were vases, figurines and antique china dishes, and you could tell that each had been set perfectly with pride into the display.

As we stood looking into the cabinet, the gentleman came over to Kenzie and asked her what she liked. Politely, she replied, "Oh, it's all really nice."

The gentleman said, "No, what do you really like?"

Kenzie said, nervously, pausing between each reply, "Well, I like that... and that... and well, that's really nice."

At this point the man gently put his hand on her forearm, smiled and looked her in the eye. He said, "You know dear, I have traveled all over the world, and met all kinds of people and the most interesting people that I have ever met, well, they know what they like." He then invited Kenzie to stand there and look, as long as she needed, and try to figure out just what she really liked.

I had moved back from where they were standing by this time and was watching her from a distance. It was like I had become invisible. As I was standing there watching them, I was thinking to myself, "Shelley, what do you really like?" If I was to have gone home right then and looked in my own china cabinet, in my own dining room, what would I see in there that I really liked? It was full of things I had gathered along the way; gifts others had picked for me and things I had inherited from loved ones. Those treasures in my china cabinet were in many ways, other people's treasures. But, of all the things in there, what did I actually *really* like?

At this point, my life had become quite dutiful. I believed I had been a good wife, a good mother, a good neighbour, a good coach; I was a really good employee and I was an exceptionally good helper. Help? I helped anyone, with anything, at any time. In fact, whatever I could do to please others by helping was what I did. But what, of all of those things, really brought me joy? I didn't really know.

Just then Kenzie said excitedly and with so much confidence, I could hear the smiling in her voice, "I like that." So, the gentleman came right over to her and took out a vase, passing it to her. It was a red vase with an ornate shape and design on it. It wasn't large, it could have fit into one of her Dad's large shoes. It had a brass base and the lining inside it was also brass. He took it from her and asked her to follow him as he brought it over to his counter. He then took out a box from a shelf behind him that had six or seven miniature replicas of this vase, all in various stages from the very beginning raw product, every step between and all the way to the finished product. It was amazing. I couldn't believe my eyes. He told Kenzie the details of each step, the time it would take to complete each phase and even the meager amount of money that the mothers, who were the makers, would be paid to create this beautiful vase. She soon knew the how, who and where in the world as well as the rarity of what it was that "she liked!" Kenzie asked questions to confirm her understanding and to soak up the knowledge he was freely giving her. Then she kindly thanked him for the time he took with her and when she was finished, he said, "You are very welcome my dear. I wanted you to not just know what you liked, but really understand what it is that you like."

As we left the store and headed out into the cold air again, we began to walk down the street and I felt as if a big change had happened inside me. You know that feeling you get when you have the urge to clean out a closet? Well, I had that feeling times a thousand. We were still holding onto one another, arm and arm but now we were holding a little tighter and walking a little lighter. I said to Kenzie, "You know, you learned a lesson today, at 16 years old, that I had not yet learned in my 40 years here. You are so lucky."

Don't get me wrong, I wasn't completely unclear. I knew there were many things in my life that I didn't like. I didn't like dishonesty, I didn't like negativity, I didn't like whining, I didn't like indecisiveness – that drove me crazy – but I knew that I did have a lot of people in my life with those characteristics. So that day, walking away from that store, I resolved to live my life with things and people in it that I *really* liked.

I want to ask you now, How do you feel? How do you really feel?

That became the mantra for how I lived my life. Figuring out what I liked became based on how things and people and even food made me feel. I'd ask myself the question after I did anything, "How do you feel?" I'd go to work and when I left as I walked to my car, I would ask myself, "How do you feel now?" I'd go for a run and then I would ask myself, "How do you feel now?" I'd go play a game with my hockey or ringette team, I'd help the homeless, do some gardening, visit with a friend... and after everything I did, I'd ask myself the question, "How do you feel now?"

What I began to learn was that some of those mundane chores that I once disliked actually made me feel really good after completing them. I loved a clean house. I loved a kitchen stocked with fresh groceries. I loved having company. I loved being alone. Lots of things that usually drained me really gave me good energy when I had completed them. I started to re-frame my thinking about those chores and they became a part of a list I kept called "The Things I Like."

I kept a pink post-it note by my phone and on that note I wrote down the question "How do you feel now?" After I spoke to anybody on the phone, I would ask myself the question "How do you feel now?" You know, it is the strangest thing when your marriage breaks down, somehow, you become this safe person for anyone you know to talk to you about how unhappy they are in their marriage. If you are separated or divorced, I know you are nodding your head now. It's really strange isn't it? I began to learn that some people called me at a time when I needed comforting, not to comfort me at all, but rather to be comforted themselves. I also began to learn that some people only ever called me if they needed something. This was a time in my life when I really had nothing left to give. After every call, I would ask myself that question and I soon learned that I liked the friends who elevated me, distracted me with stories of their day, who made me laugh, who guided me, cried with me and encouraged me, and even kicked me in the butt when I needed it. Those friends made me feel really good, so I would write their name on the list. It seemed like a natural thing that happened over time. Some people stayed and some people just faded away.

A counselor I saw once said, as you change and grow, the people around you will change and grow, too. Some of the people will change, making room for new people. Some of them will grow with you. In my case, both of those things were happening.

What I learned was that I liked honest, genuine, imperfect people. They are my favourite! If you are someone you know I would call my friend, know that you are perfectly imperfect. That's just the way I like you.

Sometimes there is a price to pay for filling your life with the things you like. Honesty, for example. I wanted to fill my life with much more of that. Getting honest with yourself means you have to get honest with others AND let them be really honest with you. That's hard for me. I am a helper by nature and to hear that I have disappointed someone, and to say no to people or to set boundaries is still hard for me.

I want to share a story with you about how getting honest can make a real difference in a relationship. To prepare for this story, I read through seven old journals and came across a writing that will best illustrate my point. It's a story about my daughter Kenzie. When she was a teenager, I had what I thought was a great mother-daughter relationship with her. Actually, I did with all three of my daughters. When Kenzie was in grade 12, right before graduation, many of her friends had already turned the legal drinking age of eighteen and were going to our local bars, but Kenzie was born in July, so she was still 17. All three of my daughters were aware that I really wanted to know them, not who they thought I wanted them to be but who they really were, and that I was working towards transparency in every area of my life. In this particular journal entry, I wrote about the time Kenzie was down-stairs in her room and she texted me to come down to talk to her. It seemed serious, so I went right down. She asked me to come in her room and sit on the bed. She quickly closed the door behind me and stood with her big eyes looking at me. She then took a big breath and reluctantly began to speak. She said, "Mom, in a few minutes Maddy and Carissa are going to come over. They will have a backpack with them. In the backpack will be a bottle of wine. We are going to have some of it while we get ready. It's called "pre-gaming" and we usually drink it from cof-fee cups, so you don't know. Then we are going to use our fake I.D.'s and go to the bar and meet up with the rest of our friends." She stopped talking and kept looking at me, her eyes even bigger now. I was silent. She then said slow-ly, "So, how's this honesty thing working for you now Mom?"

The thing is, the truth isn't always the easiest thing to say or to hear but I have learned it is always the best route.

Over time, I learned that I really liked it. I really liked let-ting my kids be perfectly imperfect. The more comforta-ble they felt really being themselves with me, the more comfortable I felt too. And the easier it was to guide them and create safe boundaries for them. We learned to laugh more, cry together and really get to know one another in an even closer way than ever before. Eventually we all shared a little more with one another, day by day.

I have also learned that there are many things I like. I have learned that I really like quiet time. That is new for me. I really like spontaneity. I like positive people. I have learned that I like being a "grown-ass woman" because grown-ass women get to own their own stories, unapologetically. I really like my perfectly imperfect modern family. Since that stroll down the street in 2008, my modern family has grown to include my three daughters, my three step daughters, my two granddaughters, my dog, **and** my two cats. I really like my first husband Al. There is nothing Ex about him. He has a special place in my heart, and he has a special place in our modern family. And, I really love my husband Paul and the respect he has for all the moving parts in this modern family.

I have been back to that little antique store to see that amazing man Selim, who, quite frankly, changed my life in a time of great adversity for me. That kind man, unknowingly, became one of the most important teachers in my life. The first time I went back, I visited on my own. It was shortly after our first encounter and I went in to purchase that vase Kenzie had chosen that special day. It became her graduation gift from me a few years later in the hopes that she would always remember the special lesson she learned from it. Selim was busy the day I went in to purchase it–likely teaching someone else one his amazing life lessons. I always wanted to visit again so just last week I went in to see him. He was there and with so many years between now and our first visit, I was so happy to see him.

It had been more than a decade since that special day. To-day he was dressed in a beautiful grey suit, white shirt and a black and grey tie. He looked as sharp as ever. There was only him in the store and another man who appeared to be his son. He had the same smile. I went over to Salim as he stood behind that same long counter and I asked him if I could share a story with him. I reminded him about that dreary day and how we had wandered into his store. I shared with him about the time he had taken with us; I told him how he had changed my life. His eyes began to well up as I spoke. I could see little tears behind his glasses that were running down the sides of his cheeks. Without responding a word to me, he came from behind the counter, took my hands in his and looked me in the eye. He then said to me, "Dear, you are making me cry. You have not just made my day, you have made my year! Come with me." He then took me over to that fine china cabinet that still stood so many years later in the heart of his store. He reached in and took out a blue vase, the same vase that Kenzie had once chosen so many years earlier. He said, "I want you to have your own so you, too, can remember how important it is to really know what you like."

Five tips to help you know what you like:

1. Take a mental inventory of the physical things around you. Do they truly bring you joy? Fill your physical space with only the things you love, even if that means more space around you and less things.

2. Really think about how you feel. Think about it after your interactions with people. Do you feel better, more energized, more relaxed, more you? Did the interaction serve you in a positive way? Does this person bring out the very best in you? Learn to spend your time with the people you really like, and you will find over time that you too will learn to really like yourself in a way you never have before.

3. After each activity, ask yourself, "How do I feel now?" It is amazing how quickly you will reframe how you feel about certain tasks or activities. Rather than the laborious task of hosting a party, going to the gym or working on a large project, you will learn to focus on the feeling after and the joy that it has brought you to complete it. Knowing that it is something you actually like, you will begin to enjoy the time you put in to completing it as well.

4. Make a list. List the <u>things</u> you really like. List the <u>people</u> you really like. List the <u>activities</u> that bring you joy. Then, do that! Spend your time and your life with the people you really like, doing the things you really enjoy, surrounded by the things you treasure. Your list will change and grow as you change and grow. Grow with it.

5. Take time every now and again to stroll. Stroll into stores you may never think to enter and learn from people you would never expect to learn from. Keep your heart and your mind open to seeing and learning about your world in a new way. It just may heal you. And, every now and then, stand in front of your own "china cabinet" and ask yourself, "What do I like? No... What do I really like?"

About the Author
Shelley Hewins Brown

Shelley Hewins Brown is a 50-year-old beautiful soul who lives, survives and thrives in North Vancouver, Canada. Shelley has overcome adversity in many forms throughout her life, as have many others. What is not the norm is Shelley's ability to seek out guidance and sanity, no matter how unpredictable things get in her world.

Shelley has spent many years working as a professional figure skating coach and has also worked in the financial services industry helping investment and insurance clients. In both cases, Shelley enjoys helping people reach their goals. Her love for working with athletes as well as young professionals sets her apart from others as she likes to work in the trenches and create a path for her clients that will help them for the rest of their lives. Her ability to work at the corporate level is not to be undermined as she has worked and contributed to many organizations and committees to improve customer service and experience in the financial service world as well as developed programs for Skate Canada and assisted, trained and guided coaches and clubs across the country to be the best they can be.

Diagnosed with a rare ovarian cancer called Adult Type Granulosa Cell Tumour only days after learning she had breast cancer, Shelley has spent the past year, when not in recovery, speaking, writing and sharing her stories to help others. Her contribution to Shine comes from a time of adversity in her life where her first marriage broke down and things felt pretty grey. She began to learn for the first time in her life; what she really liked.

Connect with Shelley:
www.heradvice.ca
Shelley@heradvice.ca
Instagram: shelleyhewins
Facebook: Shelley Hewins Brown

Two Wheels to Four: Flipping and Forgiving

By Julie Sawchuk

S ometimes you get to choose the direction your life takes; sometimes others make that choice for you. I had been a science teacher in small town southwestern Ontario for 15 years. I saw myself as a role model for young women, especially those interested in science, the environment and fitness. But after 15 years of teaching more or less the same subjects, I was beginning to wonder what would be next for my career. Would I continue teaching, change subjects, or do something completely different? At that time, I had no idea how "different" my career would become.

The year I turned 38, I decided I wanted to be more fit. My husband and I were happy with our family of four and I knew that as I aged, I would require more muscle, more activity and some kind of goal to get me there. After watching my sister-in-law race the Goderich triathlon, I decided that was my goal; I would work to complete and compete in an Olympic distance triathlon. Over several summers I worked my way up to the full distance race; 1 km open water Lake Huron swim, 42 km bike and 10 km run. I finished third in my age group (40 to 45) and I was ecstatic.

The fall of 2014, I bought my first road bike -- I couldn't wait for the next racing season to begin! For the next six months, I got up early four to five days a week to train at the pool, in the gym, on the ski trails, the sideroads and even on the track at the high school. I loved the feeling of getting up early to meet a group of friends to do a workout, and it didn't really matter what it was as long as we broke a sweat together. Coaching the Nordic ski team after school meant double workouts and I got to eat whatever I wanted.

My husband Theo and two kids Ella and Oliver were supportive of my goal. As a stay-at-home dad, Theo was accustomed to getting the kids on the bus in the morning (as I was gone by 6 am or earlier), doing the shopping, cooking, laundry, managing our tiny farm and doing all the after school running around. Although we had talked about it, I had not yet realized how much he was sacrificing so I could pursue my fitness goals and work full time.

The incident

July 29th, 2015 was a beautiful sunny morning. While sometimes I would ride with a training group, this morning I was on my own. The race was one month away, and I was feeling ready; I loved the speed of my new bike. About halfway through my 80 km ride, a car passed me deliberately so closely that I could feel the wind from his side mirror on my back. That turned out to be the last thing that I remembered about that ride.

A short time later, on the last leg of my ride (20 km from home on the very road where we live), I was hit by a car from behind. I flew 30 feet through the air and landed in the ditch of a farm field. I don't remember what happened after that, but I do know that my helmet saved my life. Several drivers stopped, including the one who hit me. They tried to keep me calm and lying still because apparently, I was trying to get up. When I arrived by ambulance at the local hospital, they knew that my injuries were out of their league.

Meanwhile, Theo and the kids had been called and he was able to see me for a few minutes before I was transported by air ambulance to London's Victoria Hospital Critical Care Trauma Unit. Getting into that helicopter scared me so much that it must have woken up my consciousness enough to store it in a different place. It was terrifyingly loud and for several weeks I reacted with tears every time I saw or heard a helicopter fly over the hospital.

When I regained consciousness after several hours of surgery, I had chest tubes and an IV and I was attached to a ventilator as well as several other machines. I was also frightened, but Theo, my parents and my brother were there to hold my hand. In critical care, the drugs that are meant to take away pain do funny things to your head... the machines designed to keep you alive are too loud to let you sleep, and other sick and potentially dying people behind the curtains turn a room meant to preserve life into a scary space. The blurred line between awake and not really awake created a time of tears, confusing conversations about what had happened, what was wrong with me and what was next.

The surgeons explained to us that I had sustained multiple injuries. Plastic surgeons repaired my forehead, chin and nose. Spinal surgery fused my spine to support the two vertebrae that were fractured; one of those bones (T4) shattered into so many pieces that a fragment damaged my spinal cord. Other bones and skin would heal with time and surgery, but not the spinal cord itself. Nerves are like electrical wires. If you cut them, no power gets through. I have paralysis from the chest down and will need a wheelchair for the rest of my life.

The hospital was 1½ hours away from home and my children (who were with their other grandparents) would not see me for almost a week. My husband, parents and siblings slept in the lounge waiting for news and time to comfort me. It was the beginning of what would be three months in hospital. A long time away from everyone and everything that gave me comfort.

It wasn't until much later that I realized how lucky I was to still have my hand function. As soon as I was able to, I started to write. Here is one of the first posts from my blog.

"Unknown" Aug 16, 2015

Here I am, standing on the edge. I am not sure what I am on the edge of, but I can tell that the only direction I can go is forward. I look behind and can see faces, places and things that I know, but there is no way to go back to them. Like some kind of video game with no reverse button, you can only go ahead, not knowing what zombies or creepers are around the corner. There is no choice but to look ahead, even though all there is is blackness -- no shapes, no figures, no light.

So, what is one to do? There really is no choice but to go forward. So, I try, but it's hard. I cry because I miss what is behind me that I no longer can reach. I imagine what it would feel like to go ahead into the darkness and slowly I do, eyes closed to concentrate as hard as I can, fighting to make my way.

And somehow, I do it, I move forward. Likely because of sheer grit and wanting to prove my strength and stubbornness, even if it is just to myself. [No, I do NOT need that chest tube back in my body, my O2 "sats" are 100%, thank you very much.]

I open my eyes to that blackness. Knowing that they are quite capable of playing tricks on me [hello crazy hospital drugs] I don't really believe what I am seeing. My guess is that they are fireflies. You know how you see them at night in early summer across the field? You think you see one, and then it's gone? Then you see another, and it disappears too? But then, when you let your eyes relax and stop looking so hard, you see that the field and the sky are actually full of them?

That is what I see now, the darkness with a few sprinklings of light. Then there are more, and more. I don't will there to be more, but they just keep coming. Somehow, they are there, and they make that darkness less scary, less unknown and more manageable.

I now know their source. The lights come from everyone sur-rounding me, both physically and virtually. And I don't even know all their names. It's crazy, because the lights just keep lighting. They are the cards, e-mails, texts, tweets, the Face-book messages, posts and reposts. They are the 4J campaign, the hugs, the food, the coffee, the time you spend with my kids and the kind words you say to my husband. They are the words that say "Share the Road" everywhere. They are the turtle. They are my family.

These lights all make me cry. Not from sadness and loss, alt-hough sometimes that does creep in; I cry from the sheer overpowering emotion of being loved. And in this powerful emotion, it makes the unknown go away.

Rehab sucks -- but it does get better

All included (recovery and rehabilitation), I spent more than three months in hospital. That was a very long time to be away from my family, friends and home. It was also a very long time to have NO personal space whatsoever. I was in a ward room with three other women, all with var-ious levels and severity of spinal cord injuries. As the days turned to weeks and weeks turned to months, I became the most "senior" in the room. I learned a lot in that time; one can't help but hear what conversations are happening on the other side of the curtains.

The three months at Parkwood Institute (a rehabilitation hospital with a spinal cord injury treatment unit) was where I had Lisa as my charge nurse. She was known to say, "I don't get paid to do it for you, I get paid to watch you do it" -- a true rehab nurse. I learned how to empty my bladder with a catheter, manage my bowels, check my skin (because I can't feel if something is wrong), get dressed and transfer from bed to wheelchair. I had no idea what paralysis really meant. Not walking is just the tip of the iceberg. I was taught how important it was for me to learn to be independent, so I didn't have to rely on some-one else for the rest of my life. I also learned how heavy legs are, how long the nights are when you are missing your family and what hard work really feels like.

My physio team called me "110" because even when they wanted me to try a movement with just a little bit of effort (like 60%), in order to focus on one group of muscles, I would use everything I had -- even my face -- to try and get those muscles to work. Physio was a place that I could, on one hand, work hard to get things back to normal. On the other hand, at physio, I was constantly reminded that I could not even sit up without help or support. I had to make lots of small, realistic goals, like getting dressed and doing my hair. I also wanted to be able to sit cross-legged on the floor to play with my kids. I eventually met that goal, and many others that I made along the way.

Three and a half years later, I can do push-ups and planks from my knees, I can stand at a walker with only my knees supported and I can almost do a sit-up. Everyone said recovery would take time. Time. Oh, how I hated hearing that word. Even though they were all correct, I wanted it to happen right then and there. Three years lat-er it's still happening. I am still recovering.

Waiting, but not waiting

Three years ago, I started saying "within 10 years, medical research will be able to repair paralysis" and I do believe it will happen. That is why I am working hard to keep my body fit. I want to be a candidate -- I will be in line and when they see me, they will say "you're next". When you have a spinal cord injury, the more fit you are, the easier it is to transfer, balance, cook, dress, put on shoes, blow dry hair and pick something off the floor. The stronger you are, the easier life is, and the less energy life consumes. Although I am waiting to get in line for that "make my legs move again" surgery, I'm not waiting sitting still.

Flip it

I don't really remember any one doctor or nurse telling me that I was paralyzed. I think that ever since I was lying in that ditch, I knew. When Theo saw me at the hospital in Goderich the first thing I said to him was, "Oh my God, I am so sorry". What I said next was that I could not feel my legs. You don't have to be a biology teacher to know that means paralysis.

I do, however, distinctly remember the two different doctors who gave it to me straight. I know where I was, what room, what bed, how they were standing and what they said. One, after three weeks in hospital said, "If you don't have it [feeling or movement] back by now, you won't get it back". I stopped listening after that. The second one, when I asked him to give me a number, said "12%". The likelihood of recovering my ability to walk, considering what strength I had gained after three months in rehab, my level of injury, my age and health was 12%.

Neither of these doctors had particularly uplifting news. But at some point in time, I'm not sure when, I started to say that 12 is not zero. Meaning that, at least there was a 12% chance of recovery, like 12/100 on an exam is better than zero! I think this is where I started to "flip it". Here is my blog post from that time:

FLIP IT: Oct 10, 2016

When something is presented in a negative way, flip it. Make it positive. Draw it out so that whatever is being said changes from bad to good or from a put down to a lift up. Every so often I run into someone that I have not seen for a while (or since the collision) and they say how it's "good to see you out". Like I'm not supposed to be out? I suppose it is possible that some people would choose to give up (I have had my moments), but staying in is just, well, boring.

I get out alright. On Saturday the kids and I went to market (again), the last outdoor market of this season. Even though I know this is silly, I felt like it was my last chance to get fresh local food. So my fridge is now full -- I think I bought three broccoli -- it all looked so good.

This is where I was when another "it's good to see you out" happened. I know it is meant well; really, I do. But how about just saying hello and asking how I am or how my recovery is going? So, this is where I have to try and flip it. They mean well; they are just concerned for my well-being and are not sure otherwise what to say. I say that I do indeed get out, a lot, and then I tell them what I want them to know: how my recovery is going and what we have been up to.

I think that Ella is starting to get tired of me flipping situations that she tells me about. I got told to "stop lecturing me" when we were talking about situations at school. You know, the kid who is kicking and screaming their way down the hall to the principal's office? We don't know what is going on in their lives, what home is like, etc. I'm just trying for empathy -- which I know she has a lot of -- but as a parent, it's my job, right?

Oliver started going to karate lessons about four weeks ago. I went to watch last week. He got his Gi for the first time and ran to put it on -- so excited, he just threw his shorts into my lap and ran to join the group. At the break, he came over to see me and said "Mom, I feel so powerful in this!" When we went out to the car, I told him that it was evident that he had learned a lot in the past few weeks and that I remember doing a lot of what he had learned. We had karate lessons when we were kids; I think we even went with my Dad for some period of time. I remember it being hard but satisfying at the same time.

I told Oliver that I wished that I could do it with him. At this point I was keeping my voice steady, trying not to show the emotion I was feeling. He didn't even miss a beat: "Well, you can still do it with your arms -- you can do it sitting on your plinth!" Of course I can. That's the thing with adults -- we get stuck in our ways (like parking in the same spot every day), not even trying to think outside the box. And here is ten-year-old Oliver, without even stopping to think about it, flipping it. Making anything possible.

So try it. Next time someone (or even yourself) says something negative, flip it upside down. Say how you want to be, not how you don't want to be. Give it/them the benefit of the doubt. Stop being negative and start being positive. It is hard, and you'll forget (I do) sometimes. But you'll feel better each time you try. I do.

I am still trying to practice this, because it is a practice. Flipping it will always take effort. But the more you do it, the better you get (just like shots in basketball). Don't just "flip it" with strangers; I have been practicing on those closest to me -- Theo and the kids. I try not to assume I know all that is going on in their heads, and all that has gone on with their day. Take a breath, stop a beat and think, "What is going on here?" and flip it. As a problem solver by nature, I have always jumped into that mode when people oppose me or present me with a situation that needs a resolution. Changing my first reaction has helped them, and me. It means not going to that "oh, this is what you should do" place which they don't usually want to hear, anyways. They want to know that they have been heard, and they want their feelings acknowledged. It also helps me to get to know them better. Yes, my husband and my kids. After 25, 15 and 12 years, I am practicing getting to know them better.

Forgive yourself

"Oh my God, I'm so sorry." Although I can't say how often, I think about what I said to Theo. I also know that I have apologized to him many times since that day. In the back of my mind, all of this is my fault. All the 'what ifs' that play through my mind -- if I had gone to the pool instead, if I had been riding with a group, if I had had a flashing light or a bright orange vest, taken a different route, or not been training at all, but instead at home with my family. All of those things were my decisions to make. I apologized to Theo because getting hit by a car did not just change my life, it changed his, and that of our kids and our families. Changed forever. I have been working on forgiving myself, stopping the 'what ifs' and getting on with recovery and life.

Forgiving myself is one thing, but being able to forgive the person whose carelessness just about killed me... that was hard. People have wanted to know what happened to the driver, and if I had ever heard from him. All I know is that he was charged with "failing to give enough room on the left while passing". A charge that he pled guilty to and no, I have never heard from him.

It has taken time, and an unexpected conversation with the officer who attended the scene of the collision. That conversation gave me a different perspective on that day, and I realized that I needed to forgive him in order to move on. I wrote about it afterwards, for the first time blogging from a different perspective.

A different perspective: Sunday July 7, 2017

Twenty-three months ago, a man, driving a car, caused a collision. It was just after 9am; he was returning home from dropping off a couple of videos in town and had stopped to get coffee and a sandwich. As he drove along the straight stretch of road that he had driven a thousand times before he felt and heard, more than he saw, something hit his car. He thought, at first, that a deer had come out of the ditch and run into the side of his car. As he looked into his rearview mirror, instead of a deer what he saw was the blur of colours, a person, flying into the ditch.

He pulled over as quickly as he could and went back to see if this person was okay. As he got to her, he saw she had a helmet on, still attached to her head. He looked and saw a bike, white, about 20 feet ahead. She was conscious and trying to get up, she was asking for his help. He said, "Oh my God. I'm so sorry. I didn't see you". She kept trying to get up, pushing with her arms. Blood on her face. He did his best to soothe her and told her to just lie still. Another man arrived and said he had called 911. An ambulance was on the way. Someone else stopped and offered first aid. Thank God.

In what seemed like an eternity, an OPP officer arrived. The ambulance came and put the lady on a stretcher, loaded her into the back of the truck and drove away with lights and siren. Now, all the attention was on him. He felt like he was going to be sick. What had happened? What had he done? What did he remember? No, he did not have his phone. Yes, he was alone. They looked at his car. There was a white streak and scratch on the front right panel and the passenger side mirror was smashed. There was a hot coffee in the cup holder and a half-eaten sandwich on the passenger seat. No, he had not been drinking the coffee -- it was too hot. Yes, he had been eating the sandwich.

He sat in the back of the cruiser while the officer spoke to him. What had just happened? How could this be? How could he have not seen this person, a woman, on a bike? He had not seen her.

After that it was all a blur. He doesn't remember how he got home, or what he told his wife and kids. Everything would be different now. He could not look people in the eye. Could not even look at himself in the mirror. He had caused irreparable harm; damage that could not be undone. He would remember this for the rest of his life. Every day he wished he had the courage to look her in the eyes and say he was sorry, longing to be forgiven.

He had not seen her.

You are forgiven.

Forgiveness has been a way for me to heal, to move on and to be in charge. It takes a lot more energy to carry a grudge and to blame someone else for what happens in your life than it does to forgive. This has meant taking new pathways, saying yes and being brave. I have been "Miss April" in a pin-up calendar, appeared on CTV news (many times) and written a monthly column for The Citizen (the local paper). I won Be Bold for Change from the 2016 Huron County Inspiring Women Awards, I met Prime Minister Justin Trudeau, I became a Rick Hansen Ambassador speaking to groups across southwestern Ontario, and I qualified as the second person in the province to be certified as a Rick Hansen Foundation Accessibility Certification Assessor. Together, Theo and I have designed and overseen the construction of a home that will be a model of accessibility and universal design. I have chosen to move on with my life.

Once a teacher, always a teacher

As a rural accessibility advocate and professional, I have travelled, lectured and written -- not just about accessibility -- but about being a patient, the importance of self-advocacy, sharing the road and that a little perseverance and some kind words will take you a long way. I have become so much more aware of the fact that everyone has something to contribute if you just allow them the opportunity to do so. My friend Chris puts it so clearly: "my satellite dish has grown". I have made friends with people that I would never have even met.

I am continuously working to help educate people about why accessibility matters. How everyone, at some time in their lives, will need a bigger washroom for maneuvering, a ramp instead of stairs, colour contrast along the sidewalk, a grab bar to steady themselves and better acoustics in a restaurant. Accessibility is about safety, independence and the preservation of personal dignity. Everyone deserves it. I have run workshops for builders, homeowners, businesses and students, spoken to youth and written about how much energy is consumed by someone with a disability just to live, let alone have a job, eat out or travel. People who disregard accessibility most often do so out of ignorance, plain and simple. They just don't know.

Ignorance also comes into play when talking about a spinal cord injury. It's not just a matter of not being able to use my legs. All the other body parts below the injury line don't work either, like the bladder and bowels. There is also a complete (or incomplete) lack of sensation -- including sex. Try pulling up your pants while sitting on them! Wheeling up an angled slope in a gravel parking lot in the rain takes a great deal of balance and energy. Explaining what nerve pain feels like is very difficult, and understanding how a urinary tract infection can make you so sick -- with no real symptoms -- potentially leading to kidney failure. In these times, depression can take you to some dark places.

Dark days, darker nights: Jan 7th, 2017

I have started this post many, many times, but mostly in my head. I have not actually been writing because, frankly, I have nothing to say. Nothing good, that is. I did not want to write about how crappy I felt, how absolutely miserable, full of pain in my body and darkness in my mind I have been for the past months. Feeling like there is no way I can continue to live like this. It was just not possible. So, I didn't write. Because this is what it has been like.

Barely able to make it to bed before falling apart, usually in tears. UTI after UTI. I scarcely remembering what it felt like to not have an infection, to not hurt. To have my feet feel like they are immersed in a bucket filled with icy water. Or the nights the nerve pain made my feet felt like they were squeezed into size 6 shoes for a full day (I wear an 8). My T4 line pain like a burning hot belt pulled tightly around my chest -- to the point where I could feel every breath, every heartbeat all the way around. Cancelling appointments. Doing nothing that I didn't absolutely have to do. Nothing but watching Netflix and sleeping until 11 am - so not me.

Pain sucks the life out of the living.

All the while I am trying to understand, to figure out, why do I feel so awful? I had many months of feeling "good". Why, now, is the pain so bad? What is different? What did I do/not do that I should/shouldn't have done? What did I eat that I shouldn't have? Is it the weather? Is it an infection? What am I not doing that I should be? And worst of all, is it all in my head? It is known that thinking of pain makes the pain even more pronounced. Am I bringing this all on myself? And then my head goes down the road to the future...how will I ever do the things I have planned: travel, work, contribute to society? How?

Dark days and even darker nights. I last, without tears, until about 8pm. After that all bets are off and you would not want to keep me company. Christmas didn't even cheer me up for long.

So, what's the deal?

I have no idea.

I have taken no fewer than three urine samples for analysis. All were negative. What? Yeah, right. Try again. I got to the point of saying, "when you dip it, it will be negative. You have to do a CNS (plate it) and it will grow something." Here I am, telling the professionals how to do their jobs. I was beginning to feel like a real pain in the ass. Twice to emerg. A total hypochondriac. I knew something was wrong. I could feel it. BUT because my body is so fucked up, it could not tell me what was going on. What was wrong.

Guess what?

I still don't know.

My doctor called yesterday, and we had a good chat. No infection. I no longer feel like a hypochondriac, nor a pain in the ass. But I still have no answers. I think I am coming out of this darkness. I think this only because I have felt okay for three days now. Not three in a row, mind you, but three out of at least 30. I keep a calendar where I track pain and meds and any crazy shit that my body does. I was, back in November, tracking the days that I had particularly bad nerve pain. Well, I stopped tracking the bad days and instead tracked the good days, which was easier to do. Because there were none. Back at that time the pain was the effect of infection after infection. Three in fact, back to back. So naturally in the end of December, I assumed that's what it was.

Now, I think that it was a virus. Or maybe an allergic reaction to the antibiotics (as would explain the hives that have come every night for the past two weeks) and goodness knows my poor gut is feeling the effects of those.

So now I am trying to make my head think that I am coming out of this darkness. I have to be. It was one (maybe two?) months out of 18. I'm no mathie, but in the grand scheme of things, that's not a large ratio. It is so hard to find perspective. The gains are small now compared to what they were at the beginning, and lord knows my expectations are still high, but good things, improvements, are still happening. It's just hard to see them. Hard to remember them.

That's where my people come into play. To give me love. Hugs. To remind me that things are happening, getting better. Stronger. Like how, just in the past five days, I have been able to stand in my standing frame without my head spinning (hardly at all). I still need my people. I can't do this alone and my poor family, well they need love and hugs too. What am I saying? Everyone does.

It's funny how writing helps. I manage to spin all these thoughts in my head into words. Words that, in order to reflect accurately what is in my head, should be dark and scary. More so now than ever. But here I am, again, trying to find something good. Flipping it. Do I do that because I am writing and others are reading? Or do I do that because I know it will help me feel better? Maybe a bit of both.

And, now I will remind myself that the sun will come again.

It can't stay dark forever.

(I wish I could remember this when I need it most.)

Putting it on the shelf

Finding ways to get out of the darkness is different for everyone. Writing helps me. Together, Theo and I are learning to share more of these dark times with each other. We've both had them. We take them out, talk about them and put them on the shelf. I have actually started saying that: "I'm putting this on the shelf" which helps get it out of my mind. Then, as I heave my body into bed, I say to Theo, "Tomorrow will be a better day, right?" He always says yes, and he's (almost) always right.

Good Grief

I'm still grieving the life I thought I would have. I don't know if I ever will stop. How is it possible for grief to be good? Grief is this crazy rollercoaster that at times you may not even realize you are on. I've had people tell me that grief is a cycle of stages that you go through. I am sure this may be true for some as they deal with a loss, but for me it has been all over the map. I think this is because I have a constant (24/7) reminder of my loss. My body travels with me wherever I go, all of it. That reminder is also there for those that are closest to me and knew me well before all this happened. Of course, I am talking about my family. Three years later we are still reminded of what was, and what is now, and the difference between them.

One of the things I have learned to do post-injury is dance. My instructor and dance partner Les had not danced with someone who uses a wheelchair, so we learned together. We have since competed in a "Dancing with the Stars" event for Victim Services Huron County and taken part in other community events to showcase wheelchair dance. Over the past year as we have learned, practiced and pre-pared, I had only shared short snippets with Theo, so he had little knowledge of what my wheelchair dance would be like. It turned out to be an emotional occasion for many and became the starting point of an important con-versation between the two of us. I wrote about it a few weeks later and our daughter Ella produced this piece of art.

Music + Movement = Dance: October 30, 2018

I knew that there was a reason why I had not written about Saturday night yet -- I was waiting for closure (and to recover). Victim Services Huron County held their 10th Dancing with the Stars dinner and auction fundraiser -- and it was amazing. Words are actually hard for me to find, believe it or not, to describe the night. I guess that is partly because it was more than just a night; it was a whole year of learning, re-hearsing and polishing something that was completely new for both Les and me.

When we first started talking about the idea of trying wheel-chair dance and competing at DWTS Huron, it was as though we were challenging each other and our own selves. Les had never danced with someone who uses a chair and I had never danced in a chair. I think we knew we were going to have fun, but, speaking for myself, I didn't know how much I would enjoy it. Fun seems like such a trite word to explain it -- but that was the word that I used most on Saturday night.

Dance was fun because it was new, but also because it was a workout, it involved music (which automatically picks you up) and it became a part of my regular weekly routine. We started dancing one hour per week, then twice, then by Sep-tember we were spending two hours twice a week working on the final "look" of our dances (of course including some time for coffee).

I have stronger core muscles now than I did a year ago. Go ahead -- try and push me over. As my friend Melissa said to me today, "You were defying gravity!" Dance has also helped me improve my posture. I have a new, lower, backrest adjust-ed to be more forward, and I sit straighter than ever.

Closure came fully to me this morning. First, I received this picture from Theo's Dad. I had been hoping that someone would have captured us, dressed up and happy. Then today we talked about how he was feeling. He has been reluctant (avoiding situations that would lead to me asking) to dance with me on wheels. I had been learning and wanted him to try too, but I got nowhere. Now I know why -- he was grieving, but neither of us realized it.

Two-step and waltz were our default dances. Ages ago, before we were married, we took dance lessons as to not make fools of ourselves in front of our guests at our wedding. We had always had a good time on the dance floor, and I suspect that we both regret not getting out and doing it more often. Now we will not be able to do that two-step or waltz the way we did before. For Theo, I think this realization came on Saturday night.

Julie & Theo Sawchuk

Grief comes when you least expect it, and in ways that make it hard to understand your feelings. Now that we have talked about it, hopefully we will be able to find a way forward, together.

If I wasn't 'Huron County' famous before, I am now. I left my house once on Monday, for a short meeting in town, and ran right into people I had never met before. They had been to DWTS on Saturday night. When they saw me, they said, "Are you Julie, who dances?" I am indeed. If you heard what the judges said: "You do dance".

This is not where my story ends

I cannot count the number of people who have said, "I could not possibly have been as strong as you have". My response is almost always the same: you don't know what strength you have until you are in the midst of needing it. At some point, I will be able to go back and read through all my blog posts and be reminded of all the tough times and what I learned along the way. Even writing this chapter and going back to edit it has reminded me of what I have learned about myself, my abilities and how to get through the tough times of life. The following are some of the more straightforward things that I do -- and maybe you can too -- to get through. Because you will, and it will get better.

Wash the dishes

Years ago, I followed "The Flylady". She helps women around the world get their homes organized. The one thing I remember most is to always leave the kitchen sink clean and shiny. Well, that is pretty hard to do if it's full of, and surrounded by, dirty dishes! Living in a pretty tight little farmhouse kitchen is tough when you use a wheelchair. Many regular kitchen tasks I leave for others to do, like wiping the counters (I can't reach all the way back) and loading the dishwasher (I can't reach both sides without having to close it up).

But I can wash the dishes. It's not easy because water drips down my elbows and onto my lap. But that is what I do to feel in control; I know that I am making a difference for my family and it gives me a sense of satisfaction and accomplishment. Being grateful that I can use my hands, I just enjoy the feeling of the warm soapy water and allow my brain time to process what's been going on. If you are lucky enough to have a kitchen window to look out (or see out of) then you can watch nature or the world go by. Often it gives me time to solve little problems (like what's for dinner); other times it's just time to think about nothing at all.

Thinking about nothing at all is hard. It takes practice. Sometimes it takes doing something like just looking at the soap bubbles attack the grease on the water, then bringing your mind back to those bubbles every time it wanders away... One thing for sure is that washing the dishes always makes life better. Fewer dirty dishes, more counter space and just room to breathe. The other thing about doing the dishes is for sure everyone will leave you alone, especially if you make it known that if they come into the kitchen to bug you, they will be handed a tea towel!

Just do it

I have a piece of exercise equipment called FES -- Functional Electrical Stimulus. It's an expensive piece of therapy machinery designed for people with loss of motor nerve function, like MS or a spinal cord injury. It uses electricity to "charge" the muscles to work. Electrodes attach to your legs (or arms) and power the muscles to move in a pattern, like riding a bike. It takes about 20 minutes to set up and each session is usually an hour. Then there is take-down time. All in all, it takes an hour and a half for one workout.

I also have to factor in bladder timing, which cannot be put off, and I'm literally stuck. Being organized enough to get on my FES bike takes some doing, and many days it seems like a pretty tall task. I've come to the realization that if I don't do it in the morning, then, generally speaking, it doesn't happen. Sometimes I try to tell myself that I will do it later in the day, or will ride with the kids in the evening if we all watch a movie, but that rarely happens.

Mornings are when I have more energy, both physical and mental. What really makes exercise happen is when I plan the night before that I am going to ride. I'll get my yoga pants out, put them beside my bed and then they are there, ready to ride in the morning. When I do ride, not only do I get the physiological benefits of having done the exercise (reducing muscle atrophy, improving circulation) but also the psychological benefits. Endorphins are wonderful chemicals, and as far as I am concerned, the more the better. They last longer than coffee, they lift your spirits, make you smile and you sleep better. When I have a series of days that I don't do any exercise, I notice.

The best message I can give myself (and you) is to just make it happen. Find the time, the headspace and, if necessary, ask for help. I can let my family know what my plans are, they can hold me accountable, or, at least they will know where I am in the morning when they can't seem to find me in bed.

Trust your gut

When you have a chronic injury or illness, your body needs a certain amount of TLC. Listening, I mean really listening, to what your body is trying to tell you, is critical. The more you know your body pre-injury, the better you will be able to listen post-injury.

Even though it's been more than three years since the incident, I am still learning to read the signs, and what my body is actually trying to tell me. Lack of sensation below my chest makes things like fatigue, a UTI or some kind of skin issue hard for my brain to understand. In other words, I don't know what is wrong. I have learned that I cry and feel desperately depressed when I have a UTI, my nerve pain ramps up with fatigue and I get chills when I have a skin issue (like sitting on a bobby pin). If you can learn what your body is trying to tell you (it's a great idea to write things down so you can see a pattern), then you'll know better when it is time to push yourself and when it's not.

This past summer I signed up for, and looked forward to, my first triathlon as a para-athlete. Leading up to the race I knew that my body was off and that I had not trained enough. I withdrew about a month before the race and, in the end, I figured out I had had yet another UTI. If I had pushed myself to do the race, I would have extended my recovery time both from the physical exertion and the infection. In fact, I'm not even sure I would have been able to finish. It turned out that Lake Huron was VERY cold that particular day and I may have done even more harm.

Cut yourself some slack

Making the decision to pull out of the race was a tough one. I talked to Theo about it. I knew I would finish; the distances were not long, and there would be tremendous personal satisfaction. But there were the possible complications like super cold water, trouble in the sand on the beach and a long recovery time. I was doing it for me, and no one would think any less of me if I didn't do it, which shouldn't have mattered anyway. There is a point at which more physical activity is detrimental to your body. It's just a matter of learning to read the signs.

Know when to take a nap

When I first had kids, other mothers would always tell me to sleep while my kids were napping, but who ever listened to that advice? It was the most productive time of the day, the time when you could get all the things done that you couldn't do when your baby was up! Well, now my body is my baby because I am still recovering. The problem is that my head is still my head and it's constantly full of things to do. There is a never-ending list that scrolls constantly and crossing something off only adds three more things.

Tell yourself that it is okay to nap. Everything will stay the way it was; things that need to get done (like dinner) will eventually (either by you a little bit later, or by someone else) or they won't, but in the end it will be okay. So just do it. Pull back the covers (if you even made the bed) and crawl in, or pull a blanket over yourself on the couch. But give yourself permission, because it's okay. And you will thank yourself later.

Put yourself first

You have to be your own advocate because no one else will do it for you. Somewhere in the past three years, I had a conversation that made me realize that I am in the driver's seat. Don't let people just shuffle you along, fitting you into all the little tick boxes on their clipboard. It's not easy to do. Put yourself and your needs first by being firm and speaking up. Ask for what you want and need. When I went to the hospital suspecting an infection (because blood in urine is not normal) I was turned away. They said, "Your urine dipped negative, so you do not have an infection". It's my body. No one knows it better than me. Please listen, because it is speaking loud and clear.

My Peeps

The best way I know to lift up my spirits and quiet my mind is to spend time with my people, who I affectionately call "my peeps". I always go away feeling whole again, reaffirmed that what I am doing, thinking and where I am going makes sense. Because that is what your people do for you. Who are your people? I guess in technical terms, it would be called Peer Support and who they are depends on where you are in life.

Peer support may be the other parents in your baby group or they may be the people you work with. For me, my people are fellow SCI survivors. When you sustain a spinal cord injury, the body changes in ways that you can't even imagine. In simple terms, it just stops working. It's not about just not being able to walk. When everything is so messed up, it is reassuring to talk to others who are dealing with the same issues. It's an instant bond. You can meet someone and within the hour you will be talking about your bladder and bowels. Everything is on the table, even sex. These are not conversations you would normally have with strangers.

Hangin' with my peeps gives us time to compare notes and laugh about things that are just plain crazy to anyone else. When I was in rehab, I had a visit from a friend of a friend who was the captain of the Team Canada wheelchair rugby team. He'd been injured more than 20 years earlier, and at a higher level (C-spine). I watched with awe as he transferred out of his wheelchair into a regular chair. He told me about the business he ran, his travels, about driving and what it had been like to be in rehab 20 years ago. Like a little kid, I asked if I could wear his Paralympic medals around my neck. He gave me hope.

That's why you need to find your people. Realizing you are not alone is sometimes all you need to keep going. It helps to hear that someone had a bowel accident worse than yours, what the tricks are to getting a front row seat on an airplane and how to travel safely with your wheelchair.

I leave you with this... Find your people and share your story. Put yourself first and just do it. Trust your gut and know when to take a nap. Forgiveness is a practice, but remember that you need to cut yourself some slack. When all is in chaos, wash the dishes.

About the Author
Julie Sawchuk

They say that life changes in the blink of an eye and that you never see it coming. There is no better way to describe what happened to Julie Sawchuk. Hit by a car in 2015, she sustained a spinal cord injury that caused permanent paralysis. Julie knows better than most that recovery is hard and how far you get depends on how hard you work. She writes from a place that is part of her own emotional therapy, but mostly because she wants to share what she has learned along the way.

Julie, a former high school teacher, is now an accessibility strategist. Julie is currently writing a book for Spinal Cord Injury Ontario to create "Road map to recovery - a guide for spinal cord injury recovery" and her next writing project will be about building a wheelchair accessible home. Julie lives in rural Southwestern Ontario with her husband Theo and their two kids.

Connect with Julie Sawchuk at
http://juliesawchuk.ca/blog

CHAPTER THREE

The Importance of Self Belief

By Rosalind Ferry

I've always thought of myself as self-sufficient. And that's largely because, growing up in Kenya, East Africa, I had to spend a lot of time on my own, without 'helicopter parents' hovering over me. My father would warn me of the hazards to be on the lookout for, including poisonous snakes, deadly spiders and venomous stone fish. He would keep a watchful eye but leave me to fend for myself, even though as a teenager I was a bit short-sighted.

I particularly recall one camping trip our family took to the Maasai Mara Game Reserve, which was always teeming with wild animals. We were on our own in every sense of the word. If we got stuck or our van broke down, we had to sort it out ourselves. There was no one else to call for help. We never took guns with us for self-defense, relying only on our wits and an innate sense of optimism.

That evening, we carefully chose our campsite, erected a heavy canvas tent and parked our Land Rover at one end, for security's sake. Soon, my mother had our favorite chicken soup warming on the fire, while my father, brother and I waited patiently on our respective camp beds, reading and chatting. Then, for some reason, I decided to look out of the tent... at the very same moment a lioness walked by the front of the vehicle.

"Daddy, Daddy, I've just seen a lioness," I whispered frantically. My father did not believe me. But I was so insistent that he took the light down from the tent's ceiling and walked out to take a look for himself. He immediately retreated. "My god, you're right. Into the Land Rover all of you!" he ordered. And into the four-by-four we launched ourselves, my father first... and my mother last. We exhaled heavily, steaming up the windows, feeling relieved we were safe, but horrified that a dangerous animal had come so close at a time when wild creatures tended to be very shy of humans. The big cat lay down by the side of the tent and played with the guy ropes. Then, she sidled over to the fire, pawed at the thick metal saucepan filled with soup and knocked it over before slinking off into the dusk. So much for the popular theory that wild animals were afraid of fire! We were all terrified to go back into the tent for the night, so the four of us lay like sardines in the vehicle and slept fitfully but safely.

In the morning, we found our cooking pot, located a long way from our tent. It had holes in it just like bullet holes -- the result of a visit by bone-crushing hyenas. So, my initial instincts were correct and helped save our bacon. If we'd remained in the tent and managed to escape the lioness, we might well have had to confront an equally formidable predator. This taught me an important life lesson: Believe in yourself and what you see, even when others don't.

You're Not That Stupid

I remember my first day of kindergarten as one of my worst days ever. The little school was a 10-minute stroll from my home in Thika, a town located at an altitude of 5,000 feet in Kenya. I walked with my best friend who lived down the road. Our teacher was a small, elderly French woman. My mother told me she liked her and even played bridge with her, which was why mother found it hard to believe that this teacher literally became a demon when she got beside the blackboard.

I was a very shy child. On my first day of kindergarten, the teacher asked us each to name a letter of the alphabet, which she would scratch onto the board with her chalk. The board became filled with letters. Then, the teacher called us out one by one to say who had chosen each particular letter. When it was my turn, I froze and was unable to answer her question. She then turned into a maniac, swore at me in French and told me I had to stay in at break time as punishment for not remembering.

Later, when I was sitting all alone in the classroom and everyone else was playing outside, she said, "If you want to go and join your friends, you can climb out of the window." I did not do this, horrified that I was being humiliated in this way and made to feel stupid. This experience badly shook my confidence for years, as I continued to wonder whether other people would discover that, deep down, I was really not that bright. Indeed, it's only been recently, after accomplishing several of my life's goals, that I've realized I'm not so inept after all. And it's a pity that it took me so long to realize this fact.

Bullying and other intimidation often leave terrible scars. But hurtful, belittling remarks say more about the person using them than those who are their target.

Passion and Tragedy

My parents decided to send me to boarding school in northern England at the age of 12. I suffered from gut-wrenching homesickness, but I did make two wonderful girlfriends, with whom I'm still in touch to this day. My parents allowed me to have one extra-curricular activity, and I chose to go horse-riding once a week with girls from my school. Sometimes we rode in a horse arena, and sometimes out on the roads and country trails. One afternoon, while on the road, a fellow rider fell off her horse and hit her head on the curb. She died instantly. I wasn't immediately aware what was happening because I was preoccupied with trying to control my horse... who was following yet another horse that had started to bolt along the side of a busy road. It was terrifying. And all I was able to do was stay on. But I remember swerving into the traffic, and thinking whether I should throw myself off the horse's back. Luckily, I stayed on. And eventually some local workmen, seeing that I was in great difficulty, grabbed the horse's reins as it tired.

That evening after chapel, my schoolmates and I were asked to sit down, and we were told about the tragedy that had befallen our fellow rider. I felt terrible for this poor girl and her family, and cried my eyes out wondering what I could have done differently. The police interviewed us each to ask if we had been monkeying around on the horses, which of course we had not. I was asked later if I wanted to continue riding. I had no hesitation in saying "yes," despite the horror of that awful ride. And to this day, I still ride almost five times a week. I must have compartmentalized this traumatic event and not allowed it to color my world forever.

Riding horses is a risky sport, but you have to put the risks to the back of your mind. Horses are highly sensitive to fear and need to feel their rider is confident. I chose not to let tragedy overcome my lifelong passion. And that decision has been a life-saver for me. It has kept me centered as a person . . . fit and happy. It's also a passion I share with my husband.

Standing Up For Yourself

Like most women, I have had some uncomfortable moments with men. My most upsetting incident was when I was 12 years old aboard a train while on my school holiday in England. I was sitting by the window, reading a comic, eating Maltesers . . . and generally minding my own business. Three or four people, including a young man in a sports jacket, boarded the train at one of the stops and sat down in my compartment. At the next stop, all of them got off the train, except the young man. And, when the train started moving again, he tried to talk to me. I didn't want to talk to him. But he swiftly rose from his seat and sat down right beside me, putting his arm around my neck and shoulder. I leapt up like a jack-in-a-box and told him in no uncertain terms to get away from me. Rushing out of the compartment, I went down the corridor, frantically searching for the conductor. I found him and breathlessly explained to him that I wanted the young man to be removed at once from my compartment. He talked to the young man who, he said, was apologetic and had believed I was about 18 ... not 12. The conductor then asked me if I wanted to press charges against the man. I replied that what I wanted was for him to be as far away from me as possible. My mistake seemed to be that I looked older than I was -- even though I was dressed as a child, in my red skirt, Norwegian sweater and red, knee high socks. For years after, I was always afraid that I might wind up alone in a train carriage with some predatorial man. But I knew that, if that ever happened, I would be so ready for it. Standing up for yourself is never wrong.

Career Path

Aged 14, I had flown home from boarding school in the UK to Kenya for my summer holidays. I remember sitting on the floor in my bedroom, very relaxed after having been out riding, and taking out a book on careers from the bookcase. I started rifling through the book and found myself in the medical section, where I was drawn instinctively as my father was a doctor and my mother a nurse. Initially, I had wanted to be a vet, but my father talked me out of it. He saw me as tall and lanky and asked me, "Do you really want to have to throw bulls on the ground, and be called out at all times of the day and night?" I did know, however, that I did not want to be a doctor, as my math skills were weak and I didn't want to kill my patients by giving them the wrong dosage of medicine. Also, I did not want to be a nurse. As my mother noted, "There are too many bed pans and too many very sick humans." When I read about physiotherapy, though, I became very excited. That profession seemed a good fit, helping people recover from all manner of injuries and conditions through physical means. The phrase in the career book that resonated most with me was one about "motivating" people. I'd always liked to think of myself as an unstoppable motivator, whether playing teacher, riding instructor or bossy preacher. From that day on, I was going to become a physiotherapist. I was going to go for it.

As it turned out, it's been a great career for me and, I think, for my patients. I have loved working with people and, yes, motivating them to help themselves get stronger, fitter and as pain-free as possible. I have worked in hospitals in London, Oxford, Victoria, Vancouver, Yellowknife and latterly in my own private practice. One of the side benefits of being a physiotherapist is that I've been able to use the techniques I've learned treating humans to help my horses and other animals without having to become a vet. It's funny how you pick one direction in life and seem to wind up coming full circle to where you started in the first place.

Will to Succeed

When I was 17, my parents suggested that I might want to think of climbing Mt. Kilimanjaro in Tanzania during my summer holiday. My parents themselves had climbed Africa's highest mountain (at 19,341 feet or 5,895 metres). And I thought that, yes, it might be a fun adventure. I arrived home in Kenya from boarding school in England, got over the jet-lag and prepared to climb the snow-capped mountain with five other young people. My father showed me how, at high altitude, I would have to breathe while gasping for air. One advantage, he said, was that our Kericho home, in the tea-growing highlands of neighboring Kenya, was already at 6,500 feet (1,981 metres). So I might have a few more red blood cells to carry more oxygen. He also told me how I would walk three steps forward and slide back two, due to the loose scree. Many hikers do not get to the top of the mountain with its three volcanic cones. So I knew I was in for a real challenge.

I met up with my group in the Kenya capital of Nairobi. We then drove and stayed at a lovely little hotel at 6,000 feet. It was owned by a German lady who told us not to push ourselves too much because one of her guests had recently died after climbing the mountain -- due to cerebral oedema brought on by high altitude. This gave me the shivers. We set off the next morning. This was an organized trip, so all our food and equipment was carried up by porters, as they called them. I was wearing a pair of suede, lace-up shoes with no tread that I bought in central London. They were so comfortable to wear, but were not designed for climbing mountains. It was an arduous climb up to 9,000 feet, where we slept in a hut.

The following night, we slept in another hut at 12,000 feet. And the third day, after grinding our way grimly upwards, we were heartened to see Kibo, the plum-pudding-like mountain peak. It looked so tantalizingly close, but we still had a long way to go as we walked by giant groundsel, lobelia and along the Saddle. People in the group were beginning to struggle now, accusing me of going too fast. But I felt I was going at my own pace. Exhausted, we trudged our winding way up to 15,000 feet and the final hut where we were to eat our supper, sleep until midnight and get up before dawn to tackle the last four thousand feet.

I can remember feeling panicked in my sleeping bag, fearful that I might not be able to breathe due to a lack of oxygen. My chest felt like it had a weight pressing menacingly on it. The walls of the hut were engraved with all kinds of mad scribblings from climbers who had obviously suffered too. Three people in my group fell victim to mountain sickness and had to start going down the mountain. Only Hans, a Danish boy on his second attempt at the mountain, our guide and I made it to the top.

It was everything my father described and more. Dawn was still rising. We were above the clouds, looking across at the jagged peak of Mawenzi below. It was an ethereal sight and a moment I'll never forget. However, I was absolutely exhausted. Pulses seemed to be throbbing all over my body. In fact, the guide said to me in Swahili, "If you don't get up, you will die." I remember drinking in that incredible, unbelievable sight before the three of us quickly slid down the scree.

It took two days to get back to the hotel. My face and one side of my neck were badly burned from the sun, even though I had tried to protect my skin. The village people cheered us and made Hans and me garlands of everlasting flowers to wear around our hats to show we got to the top. I still have them to this day. And, yes, those suede shoes were the ultimate in comfort, but scored a zero for grip. I always look back on this never-to-be-repeated experience as one of the highlights of my life. What got me through it was a certain amount of competitiveness with my parents and a will to succeed.

Family Tragedy

Having passed all the necessary exams, I was accepted to do my physiotherapy training in London. Just before my final exams, I got the devastating news that my brother, who was doing a PhD at Cambridge University, had committed suicide. He had had his ups and downs over the years. But I had no idea he was so depressed that he would even consider taking his own life. Both of us had a seemingly idyllic life growing up in Africa and shared a love of animals. In fact, we were close in a number of ways. Understandably, I spent the next months grieving. It would have been easy for me, alone in a major city, to have been crushed by it all. But I realized that, for me and my parents to get over this tragedy, I would need to be as strong as I had ever been.

I passed my exams and started my career as a junior physiotherapist at the Churchill Hospital in Oxford, doing outpatient and other work. The job wasn't as I had imagined, and I felt that perhaps I had made a mistake in my career choice. I was lonely and my restlessness worsened, and I decided to take a chance and try something completely different -- by emigrating to Canada. At least that would be one way, I thought, of escaping the terrible sadness of my brother's cruel and untimely death.

Moving to Canada

Shortly after arriving in Canada, I started working as a staff physiotherapist at the Royal Jubilee Hospital in Victoria, the capital city of beautiful British Columbia. Compared with the UK, I was relatively well paid. But I remember being so busy that I could barely get through my daily caseload. For the next three years, though, I did several things I'd always wanted to do, including owning three different horses and doing show-jumping and eventing. It was a wonderful way of forgetting the sadness of my recent past.

I also got married to a young journalist man with big dreams. In fact, we soon left Victoria for Yellowknife in the Northwest Territories, a vast, heavily-underpopulated region filled with a spirit of adventure. I worked at Stanton Yellowknife Hospital, treating Inuit, Metis and people employed at the two local gold mines. Frostbite, chest infections and gunshot wounds were among the conditions I encountered. Every month, I'd fly in a small plane to communities with no physiotherapist, limited medical facilities, and seemingly endless wilderness.

One memorable Christmas, my husband and I spent a week camping with George Calef, a top wildlife biologist friend, 40 miles northeast of Yellowknife. The temperatures never got above 30 below. Everything froze if it was not within close proximity to the dumpy airtight stove in our tent. I brought Oil of Olay for my face, but the bottle froze and cracked. Ice-hardened potatoes became like lethal weapons. I remember George saying, "What would you do if you were sleeping naked in your sleeping bag and your tent burns down?" What would you do? That thought recurred many times during that week and needless to say, I slept with my clothes on!

It was a magical time. The wolves howled nearby. And we lullabied ourselves to sleep with Robert Service poems about the northern lights and the men who went mad searching for the motherlode. I felt rugged, tough . . . and that nothing was beyond me. Which was just as well. We had no radio and no backup plan if we got sick or badly wounded. Our only security was that a bush pilot would pick us up at a certain time on a certain day at the end of the trip. Which, as luck would have it, is what happened.

Shortly after leaving the north, we moved to Toronto, where I gave birth in hospital to a wonderful, healthy boy. I stayed at home to take care of him and began a knitting business with my friend across the road. We did quite well, producing little children's vests decorated with animals in spunky colors. We even landed an order from a store on Madison Avenue in New York. It was a fun venture, but one that was not going to feed us that well. Later, we returned to British Columbia where I started part-time work at Lions Gate Hospital in North Vancouver. But I became disillusioned with hospital work and got the itch to set up my own business.

One day, at the top of Mount Seymour, I made a vow to myself not to wait any longer and just to get on with it. Soon afterwards, an opportunity arose for me to start my own physiotherapy clinic in our community by the sea, Deep Cove in North Vancouver. I began this when our son was six; I was petrified and wondered how I would juggle all the demands on me. But an insistent inner voice told me I couldn't pass up the chance to fulfil a long-held dream. I became busier and busier, and hired other people to work with me – until I found a young physiotherapist who was keen to join me in a partnership. We expanded the clinic and made a successful practice, which has now serviced the Deep Cove area for more than 30 years. During that time, I have treated an amazingly interesting group of patients and felt a strong connection to the place where we chose to raise our son, who is now an aerospace engineer with his own lovely family.

Health Struggles

What's the important thing in life? Friendships, certainly. And a passion for living is obviously key. But perhaps the most underrated aspect of our lives these days is our health. Health is the perfect gauge of how well we are doing and coping. It's also wonderful in its own right. People who brim with good health radiate those positive vibrations that make others want to be our friends and to share their own passions with us. Healthy people are generally well-adjusted people who are both in balance with their minds and bodies and the world around them. But being healthy requires constant attention and often hard work.

I was a fairly healthy child, but one who became increasingly anxious. I held all my tension in my neck, jaw and ears. I lived in my head. I was plagued by some skin problems, sore throats and ear infections. I also inherited from my mother otosclerosis. She had this condition -- stemming from abnormal growth of bone of the middle ear -- in one of her ears. I had it in both. My progressive hearing loss was accompanied by tinnitus, which generated an unrelenting stream of whirring noises. It was highly debilitating. Working as a physiotherapist, I eventually had to wear a hearing aid.

Over the years I had to have four surgeries on my left ear and various tubes to compensate for a badly scarred ear drum and a tendency for my eustachian tube to get plugged if I got a cold. I remember one particular day at work feeling a cold coming on, and that night my hearing completely went. I could hear nothing, not even the shower running. I was devastated. The only way for me to get sound was when I lay my head on my husband's chest and he talked to me. I saw my Ear, Nose and Throat doctor who said I needed further surgery, involving the insertion of a miniature implant to replace the failing bone. I lay in bed feeling sorry for myself. How could a health professional who was always advising people on their health be so unhealthy? Then, the realization dawned on me. I had taken care of everyone else except myself. Well, I had the surgery and everything improved for a while but the implant later failed; it got pulled off the bone by all the scar tissue. Luckily, the highly-skilled surgeon was able to find enough space to replace it and restore some of my hearing. I returned to work. Then, later I had my right ear done. I was delighted to be able to hear better and not have to wear a hearing aid. During all this unpleasantness, I learned a lot about myself and the demons I was facing. I learned to find ways of calming myself down. Finally, I had my last hearing test. It was my surgeon's time to be surprised. He said my hearing had really improved which was partly the result of the surgery. I told him I had done a lot of work to calm myself and reduce my anxiety. He agreed that by learning how to do this would help to quieten an over-active central nervous system and brain which really does affect how we hear.

I learned how to relax through meditation, yoga, qi gong, riding and the outdoors. I also tried to resist the urge to juggle doing so many things which is quite an art when you have a career and a family. I even wrote a book about posture (The Posture Pain Fix, Prominence Publishing), which helped me focus my physiotherapy practice on posture, relaxation and vestibular rehabilitation for patients suffering from dizziness and balance disorders. In other words, my own struggles and traumas had served to help others regain their health. And that was a wonderfully reassuring thing to know. The message I want to reinforce now is that, no matter what life throws at you, don't neglect your own health. I eventually sold my share of my North Vancouver physiotherapy practice. But I was healthy enough, both physically and mentally, to be able to continue to work there for a further dozen years.

In the End

My life has been a roller-coaster of joy and pain, success and failure, cowardice and courage. My genetic weaknesses have come from my parents, but my mistakes are all my own. But one thing I have come to learn is there is always hope, however dicey things get. A positive mindset is key to overcoming the obstacles you encounter on your way. Here are eight tips for living well:

1. Listen to your gut and learn to help yourself.

2. Believe in what you see and be kind to yourself.

3. Don't let jealous people kill your dreams.

4. Set realistic goals and pursue them.

5. Enjoy quiet time to reflect, relax and refresh.

6. Look after your health.

7. Learn to master at least one marketable skill and/or exhilarating passion.

8. Be like a great bush pilot. Make sure your engine is well maintained. Keep calm, be safe, focus on a good landing spot and enjoy the adventure.

About the Author
Rosalind Ferry

Rosalind Ferry is a long-time British Columbia physiotherapist and author of the book "The Posture Pain Fix" (Prominence Publishing). Over the years, she has helped literally thousands of people with everything from sore necks, bad backs, wonky knees, balance disorders and trauma of all kinds. Her patients have included everyone from young soccer players to senior citizens with mobility issues. They have told her they appreciate her calmness, common sense, willingness to listen and holistic approach to their treatment. Her inspiration has been her love of animals and the great outdoors . . . and her enjoyment in seeing others succeed in dealing with their pain and regaining control over their lives. Her own struggle with chronic ear and hearing problems has made her empathize fully with those battling similar debilitating, complex problems. Her philosophy has been one of combining physical treatment with an appreciation of the part that stress and other psychological issues play in patients' overall health. As the Latin maxim says: *"Mens sana in corpore sano (a healthy mind in a healthy body)."*

Connect with Rosalind at: ros.ferry@gmail.com

CHAPTER FOUR

Six Months to Give

By Robin Levesque

I used to think I was lucky. After 20 years of dedicated public service, I had worked my way up to a senior management position with a six-figure income and a corner office overlooking a one-hundred-year-old green bridge crossing the South Saskatchewan River that runs through the coulees of Medicine Hat, Alberta.

As a government employee, my job was secure. My wife was working for the same employer as a friendly neighborhood tax assessor. Together with our investments, we had built a $250K per year lifestyle. We owned a comfortable home in a new subdivision. Our dream vehicles filled the two-car garage. I even bought our 17-year-old daughter a brand new car, so we didn't have to drive her back and forth to her work.

Life was good. My wife had grown up in this little city in the prairies. We had our dream jobs in her hometown and plenty of family to socialize with. Work for me was so easy, I used to joke that I could do this job in my sleep. That's exactly what happened. I fell asleep at the wheel. This comfortable little life was about to spin out of control.

We had moved to this part of Alberta from next-door British Columbia. Prior to living and working in Medicine Hat, I had been living in Victoria, while my wife and two daughters were holding up the proverbial fort back in Kamloops. Although I was able to commute back and forth between Kamloops and Victoria every two weeks, the time apart was starting to wear on our family.

At one point, we made the conscious decision that it was time for a change. We saw three options. I could move back to Kamloops. Or, we could move the whole family to Victoria. A third option was to go somewhere entirely different. We were no strangers to moving, so this didn't scare us.

During the summer of 2008, we were visiting my in-laws in Medicine Hat. After my father-in law finished his morning routine of going through the obituaries, my wife picked up the local newspaper and came across a job posting for a manager of the City's land department. "Check this out", she said. "Are you going to apply?" I responded that it sounded like a great opportunity, but it was "Medicine Hat".

Victoria after all, where I was living at the time, was the prime jewel of Canada's West Coast. It was like living in paradise on earth: beautiful scenery, mild temperate weather, and an exceptional lifestyle.

I had built a successful career as a public servant, first in the field of land development and marketing then as an expert project manager. Both fields were considered "endangered species" in the provincial government, because new post-secondary graduates were flocking to the private sector for higher starting salaries.

For this year-and-a-half, I had been part of the Project Management Centre of Excellence (PMCOE), an elite branch of government that was launched by a visionary Dale Christenson. In essence, I was an internal project management consultant and corporate trainer.

I was having the time of my life. I was getting paid to do what I loved to do, leading deep dive workshops on project management and negotiation with fellow public servants. I was flying all over British Columbia to help others transform the way they managed projects. I was meeting new people every day. In a very short time, I became a very effective trainer, often reaching 98% on overall satisfaction ratings from my workshop participants.

While I was in Victoria, I even started my own business to provide workshops to the private sector. Workshop development and delivery was my "retirement plan". It seemed to generate a decent income for relatively short spurts of time on the teaching platform. It offered opportunities for travel. Furthermore, it gave me a chance to make a contribution and give my best to the world.

Leading workshops became far more than a paycheck and opportunities to travel. It was my passion … my purpose. Even after leaving the Project Management Centre of Excellence (PMCOE) for Alberta, I continued serving clients such as Northern Health in Prince George, ProjectWorld Business Analyst World in Vancouver, Toronto and Montreal, Buildex in Edmonton and Seattle, Federated Press in Calgary, Eco-Cities in Nantes France, and Bard College's MBA in Sustainability in New York City.

PMCOE had originally been set up to help high performers transition to their next big opportunity. Medicine Hat was that big opportunity.

Back in Medicine Hat in that corner office overlooking the green bridge, I often wondered though: What would it be like to be a full-time author, speaker and trainer? I would find out when I retire and could afford to work only if and when I chose to.

I yearned to be a full-time author, speaker and trainer. Even though I still loved real estate, I grew tired of the daily grind. I had a deep desire for being my own boss and making a positive difference in the world.

I could have focused more on my practice, but the money I was making in government was too good to give up. Plus, I was building a healthy pension that would someday finance my dream business. They often refer to this combination as the "golden handcuffs". In many respects, I was sitting on the fence ... always one foot out the door.

During that time, I was introduced to the Canadian Association of Professional Speakers (CAPS) by a dear friend John Popoff. I had been mentoring John for years. He knew that CAPS was a really good fit for me. I started attending the Super Saturday event in Calgary once a month. Then I enrolled in the Fast Track program designed to teach experts who speak the business of professional speaking. So once a month, I would get up at 5:00 am for the three-hour drive to Calgary. I sat in a room with 100 of the best speakers and trainers in Southern Alberta to participate in three hours of learning best practices for professional speakers. Then I had lunch with my fellow Fast Track participants. We spent the rest of the afternoon learning tools and techniques that would change some of our lives forever.

One of the lessons I remember most from this experience is that we were asked to "pick a lane". In other words, commit. Commit to the business of professional speaking, commit to a topic, and commit to a niche. Still, I was reluctant to give up the luxury of a secure job that I could do in my sleep and earn a six-figure income to boot. Instead, I convinced myself that I lived in the land of "AND". I could continue working in my field AND dip my big toe into the pool that is the business of professional speaking.

During this time, I developed a special friendship with Tammy Komanchuck. Tammy was the Organization Development Officer where I worked. We first met over the telephone while I was still in Victoria to administer the Work Alignment Profile by McFletcher. It turns out that we both shared the profile "Project Manager" and hit it off. Once we started working under the same roof, we immediately started collaborating on developing and leading workshops for our co-workers in project management and interest-based negotiation.

We also co-created offsite retreats for my new team with a focus on strengths building, shared values and shared vision. Tammy and I even travelled to Lethbridge together to become certified trainers in Crucial Conversations by VitalSmarts. We brought that program back to our employer and trained over 100 co-workers in the art of conflict resolution.

Tammy became a mentor to me. She had been in the organization development field for two decades. She whet my appetite for attending the Cape Cod Institute to learn from world-class experts. She called me a "super-learner" and recognized my passion for learning, teaching and leading.

Also in the same period of time, I completed my Master of Arts in Leadership from Royal Roads University in Victoria. One of the highlights of that experience was sitting in the Lure restaurant at the Delta Hotel. I was facing the legislative building straight across on the other side of the Inner Harbour. It was a glorious day, and I longed to be back in Victoria for good. I made a wish ... which became an intention ... which drove part of my personal vision for the future. Someday, I would come back to Victoria and live the life of my dreams.

After graduating with my Masters, a lot of great things happened. I was invited to speak at the Urban Development Institute Alberta Conference, Canada Green Building Council Alberta Conference, Abbotsford Agri-Energy Forum, Ecocity World Summit in France, Royal Roads University Society of Leadership Conference, Building Communities That Create Health in Medicine Hat, and the Bard MBA in Sustainability in New York City. I felt like I was on fire.

It was the Royal Roads University Society of Leadership inaugural conference that opened my eyes to a whole new world of possibilities for leadership. One of the conference highlights was meeting one of my heroes Barry Posner. I made sure to go early with the intention of meeting Dr. Posner. It was a room set up for a couple of hundred people. There were only two other people in the room, so I got a great seat close to the stage. And there he was ... walking straight toward me. Dr. Posner is close to seven feet tall, so he made quite an entrance. I said good morning. He stopped. We introduced each other and had a great conversion. That was a great moment.

The most profound learning that occurred for me at the conference was the exposure I gained to the emerging fields of positive psychology and mindfulness as it applies to leadership. Positive psychology is a relatively new branch of psychology that focuses on making people happier by increasing positive emotions and decreasing negative emotions. The definition of mindfulness is "... paying attention, on purpose, in the present moment, non-judgmentally" according to Jon Kabat-Zinn.

Combined with best practices in leadership, I saw tremendous potential for a positive leadership system that could change the world.

That was the event that inspired me to finally commit to going to the Cape Cod Institute with my friend and mentor Tammy. Richard Boyatzis, another one of my superstar academic and author heroes was conducting a one-week workshop on Resonant Leadership.

After my successful encounter with Barry Posner, I repeated the same routine. I went to the workshop early. I was the first participant through the door. Professor Boyatzis was sitting at a table in the front of the room. He greeted me with a smile and asked we why I was here. I told him he was the reason I was here, that I had read his book Primal Leadership and taken his Coursera course on Resonant Leadership. This conversation would change my life forever.

For that entire week, I got to study a master presenter in action. Given that his son was my age, he had to have been in his seventies. And he was still working: 12 hours per day on university days and 6 hours per day on his days off, and loving it! I was truly inspired.

As a result of this workshop, I wrote down my new vision for my Ideal Self, a term coined by Professor Boyatzis. What would my ideal life look like 5, 10, 15 years from now? I would be retired from public service. I would have graduated from the Doctorate in Business Administration from the Grenoble École de Management in France. I would thrive as a best-selling author, speaker and trainer that travels all over the world to deliver my message. I would combine mini-retirements with learning adventures in Europe, Cape Cod, Whistler, Banff, Victoria and Nanaimo. And I would be helping my wife with her part-time catering business. Little did I know that only five months away awaited a major life change that would greatly accelerate my life vision.

It was a crisp Monday morning in early November 2014. I was looking at the green bridge and wondering to myself, What's today going to bring? What's this week going to look like? Then something happened that changed my life forever. I sat down at my desk. The phone rang. It was my relatively new boss's administrative assistant. It appeared that he wanted to see me in Boardroom A.

I grabbed my journal and made my way down to the first floor and walked through the door of Boardroom A. My boss was sitting across the table. To his right was sitting the HR Manager. And I thought to myself, No good is going to come of this. My boss could hardly look me in the eyes. After a moment of silence, he looked up at an empty space in the middle of the table. In this shaky voice he said, "Robin, these conversations are always hard, so I'll get straight to the point. We're letting you go. We think you've lost your passion for real estate development." That was it. Twenty plus years of dedicated public service... and this is where it ended.

I was shocked. Six years of developing and working with a one of the best real estate development teams in the world. Under my leadership, the Department had been featured as a best practices land developer and team at Urban Development Institute Alberta Conference, Canada Green Building Council Alberta Conference, Alberta Professional Planners Institute Conference, Abbotsford Agri-Energy Forum, Ecocity World Summit, Royal Roads University Society of Leadership Conference, and Medicine Hat Building Communities That Create Health. I even went to share my vision and mission of leadership in sustainable development at the Bard MBA in Sustainability class in New York City on my own dime.

My now ex-boss then handed me over to the HR Manager and left the room. The HR Manager went over my package and my options. He escorted me over to my office, where my wife was waiting. She looked at me with this look of fear and stress all over her face and body. "You got fired?" she asked. "Yes, but this could be the best thing that ever happened to us", I replied. When she left, I handed over my cell phone and access card to the HR Manager. I looked at the green bridge from this vantage point one last time. At that moment, the green bridge became a metaphor for the next four years of my life.

A bridge connects the end of one road to the beginning of another road on the other side of an obstruction such as a river. A bridge is part of the road network, but it's distinct. It's a relatively short distance compared to the rest of the road it connects to. And it has a very specific purpose. It's a transition from one side of the river to the other.

Have you ever experienced a sense of complete relief and anger at the same time? This is a rare occurrence reserved for a select few moments in our lives called chronic stress. These moments are characterized by the newness to the experience. Getting fired is something I had never experienced in my life or even considered a remote possibility. The outcome was uncertain. Recall that my wife and I had built a quarter of a million dollar lifestyle that included two houses, three cars and extensive travel. There was a tremendous threat to my ego. Oh no, this couldn't be happening to me! Finally, I had absolutely no control over the outcome. I couldn't even influence any decision prior to that moment in time. No one asked me for my input. There was no opportunity to negotiate.

I recovered relatively quickly. By the next week, I was teaching a class at the University of Calgary's Urban Planning Masters Program. Within a couple of months, I was teaching an entire certificate in project management at the local community college. This was the perfect segue into the next phase of my life. In one fell swoop, almost all of my five-year plan was well on its way to becoming a five-month reality. I hadn't been able to choose a path, so the universe decided for me! This was my green bridge.

During the following two-and-a-half years, I pursued my combined passion for learning, teaching and leading workshops. I joined CAPS National and its Calgary Chapter and attended several more events including a national convention in Toronto.

I continued teaching the certificate in project management and also joined the corporate training team at the college. And I collaborated with the college administrators on developing a certificate in positive leadership that we later piloted.

Life was great, but finances were tough. We sold both houses. We lost some money on the Medicine Hat house due to poor market conditions. We made some on the townhouse in Kamloops.

Our daughter had already moved out by now, and my wife and I downsized considerably. At our main house on the prairies, we filled an entire construction bin with unused items and junk we had collected over 15 years of moving around British Columbia and Alberta. We placed everything else that we didn't need for day-to-day subsistence in a storage unit.

For almost a whole year, we lived like vagabonds. We stayed for six months in the partially finished basement at my in-laws with our two dogs Bam and Chiko. Then we did the same for three months with my friend and mentor Tammy.

We were ready for a move... not sure to where, but we were ready. We did manage to narrow it down to either Calgary or somewhere on Vancouver Island. Our daughter had been living in Nanaimo for over a year, and we missed her dearly. As it turns out, the universe came calling once again.

I got a call from a recruiting firm in Vancouver. They were responding to an application I had submitted for an executive director position in Victoria. The world of real estate had opened its lucrative door for me once again. I got the job. Because most of our belongings were in storage, we were able to mobilize fairly quickly. Before long, we were reunited with our daughter. Within months, she made the move from Nanaimo to Victoria and was living in our basement. Life had made its way back to some form of normal... for now.

After only a year-and-a-half in what I thought would be my dream job, it happened again... the perfect storm.

I came to work and I met with my team to prepare for my bi-weekly meeting with my boss. I felt well prepared, but as it turns out, not for what lay ahead.

My boss showed up at my office door on time and as planned. He asked me if we could meet in a boardroom nearby. On our way, we exchanged pleasantries and asked about each other's weekend.

This scenario felt familiar. I walked into the boardroom and was introduced to a woman from HR. Now I knew that no good would come of this... again! My gut feeling was confirmed. I was terminated without cause: no reason; without cause; period.

What followed could have been the worst six months of my life. I had just lost what I thought was going to be my dream job. My marriage of almost 20 years was breaking down. We were $200K in debt. We already had to sell both our houses to pay down even more accumulated debt, essentially wiping out all of our equity. I had grown way too dependent on alcohol and nicotine for stress relief, and it was starting to affect my health. And to top it all off, my very first pet ever, a dog named Bam had fallen sick, and it was time to put him down. I was burning out... fast!

Any one of these experiences qualifies as a major life event... a significant change. Combined together, given the sequence of events and how fast everything came at me had the makings of a major mid-life crisis. I remembered what Richard Boyatzis said in Cape Cod: "If you don't have your mid-life crisis in your forties, it's going to hit you like a freight train in your fifties!"

Instead, it turned out to be the best times of my life... one of self-discovery and profound transformation. It was a time to discover "New Robin". Even though I was 53 years old, this was only the halfway mark of my life. Whatever decisions I wish I had made in the first half of my life, I could make in the second half.

My first priority was dealing with the stress of losing a job, a marriage and a dog all at the same time. I needed to nurture my spirit, mind and body. What the latest scientific research says about maximizing health and longevity is directly proportional to what we do every day ... the choices we make and how they influence our biology: sleep, meditation, exercise, breathing, eating, and harvesting positive emotions for healthy relationships.

Fortunately, I had built a strong foundation over most of my adult life. I already meditated almost every day, exercised regularly, ate healthy food and slept well. Plus, I experimented with alternative modalities for preventive health such as yoga, sports massage therapy, chiropractic treatments, reflexology, and acupuncture.

Stress was my enemy though, and I had known this for a long time. According to Deepak Chopra, "stress is a real or perceived threat ... that interferes with the spontaneous flow of cosmic intelligence". A common definition of stress in my Mindfulness Based Stress Reduction (MBSR) learnings is a real or perceived threat that we feel we are not equipped to deal with. I later discovered that it's not the stress that kills us ... it's our perception of stress.

Deepak Chopra says that stress interferes with the cosmic flow of intelligence. In one of his online course modules, I was able to quickly write down 10 moments of extreme stress and emotional pain in my life starting as early as age nine and as recent as the past two months. More on this later. Dr. Chopra says that: "Karma is a prison. Life is a flow between the banks of pleasure and pain. Without the play of opposites, there is no experience. Experience is always by contrast." I decided to test this theory.

How could I release that which did not serve me? How could I let go of limiting beliefs, negative thoughts and emotions like fear and anger, and bad habits? I sought out some extra help from some interesting resources. I signed up for SynchroDestiny with Dr. Chopra online. I joined the Transcendence master class with the Food Matters TV, also online. I am still taking Unlimited Abundance with Mindvalley. And there was the live course in Mindfulness in the Workplace at Royal Roads University.

These were all very useful, but the real transformation occurred in a one-hour coaching session with my friend and colleague Nathalie Plamondon-Thomas. She guided me through a meditation to release the fear and anger of loss in my life. It turns out that, like many of us, I had a long history of ups and downs. Sometimes you win; sometimes you lose. Although I had generally won more often than lost, I had some significant limiting beliefs and built-up anger and fear of loss. Together, we released the anger and fear caused by those 10 emotionally painful events I had identified in Dr. Chopra's course.

Soon after, my wife and I separated. We had known prior that each of us was living through a mid-life transformation. We both refused to call it mid-life crisis because we chose to remain positive and seek out the opportunities that would make this transformation possible. We both discovered that we were far better at being friends than a married couple. I didn't lose a wife, I gained a best friend for life. We now tell people in jest that we are "happily separated".

From a career perspective, I realized with the help of my book coach that I needed to work on my mindset, business knowledge and marketing savvy. This was my big chance to finally pursue my goal as a full-time author, speaker and trainer.

I was, and still am, living the "perfect day every day". Mornings started early between 5:00 and 6:00 am. I spent the first two-to-three hours of each day on self-care: pre-meditation, meditation, journaling, reading uplifting content, and learning. I would have my power breakfast and work on the business for three hours. Then I walked my dog Chiko for 45 minutes down to, and back from, the Inner Harbour. When we got home, I made and ate my power lunch. Then I would go to the local café for coffee and 90 minutes of writing. Then I had the option of writing some more or going to the local gym. All of these activities were within easy walking access. My dream vehicle, a 2014 Jeep Wrangler Unlimited sat in my driveway for weeks at a time. My daughter used it more than I did. Yes, I was living the perfect mini-retirement once again.

The fourth month into the journey is when I made a conscious decision to give for the following six months. I would give my best content to the world through my website, LinkedIn, Facebook, YouTube and Twitter. I would give my time to worthwhile causes and my first coaching clients. I would give away the first three chapters of my book to anyone who wanted it.

Around this time, I was also planning an amazing learning adventure. CAPS National Convention was coming to Vancouver in December 2018. A learning adventure for me is when I purposefully integrate all four major domains of my life when the primary purpose of a trip away from home is learning at say a workshop or conference.

I got to meet one of my childhood heroes, Rick Hanson, "The Man in Motion", in person. I got to sit down and have breakfast with Miss Canada 2018, Maria Giorlando. I mingled with so many wonderful people... experts who speak for a living. And I met Mitra Mohamadzadeh, a PhD Candidate in Human Resources who is very passionate about helping people discover themselves through self-awareness, clarity of personal vision and goal setting. We discovered that we had so much in common that we are now collaborating on a book entitled Border Crossers: Where Positive Change Meets Positive Leadership.

Looking back, that CAPS Conference was a tipping point for me. The people I met helped me become more self-aware of what I needed to do to succeed as an author, speaker and trainer. There is nothing like fully immersing yourself in your vocation for three full days.

For my journey prior to that tipping point, it was important for me to believe that there is always a light at the end of the tunnel. This too would pass. There's good in every experience. My friend Dale Christenson later compared these phases of our life as a dreary day in Vancouver. You step outside under the clouds and the rain. It's not pleasant, but you know it won't last forever. Because you know that above those clouds the sun shines bright. And one day soon those clouds will part and the sun will shine its warm rays down on you once again.

In my search for meaning, I received many signs from the universe. I was attracting everything that matched my energetic vibration. I had the strength to leave the past behind. It was time to create a new beginning and to make my decision. The words from my Fast Track training still resonated with me: "pick a lane".

I needed to allow my true individuality to wake up, channel and speak my soul's truth. I was ready to make a difference in the world, to recognize and seize opportunities all around me. All I needed to do is be open and stay positive all the way!

Hitting the perfect storm of life a second time in less than four years was my ultimate wake up call. The universe was telling me to pick a different green bridge, maybe a blue bridge. It was a time of deep transition. One day, I could help people that go through their own transitions in life: careers, businesses, mid-life and beyond.

There was a noticeable threshold between the end of 2018 and the new beginning that is 2019. My intentions for 2019 are posted on the wall next to my fridge. I look at them every day.

I have great spiritual, mental and physical health. I am in the best shape of my life spiritually, mentally and physically. I have great relationships. My ex-wife and I are best friends. My special bond with my youngest daughter has grown to a whole new level. She is my rock.

I am building the business of my dreams as an author, speaker and trainer. This includes working on my first of many best-selling books, Resonate to Co-Create: a Transformative Learning Adventure Into Positive Leadership. My company DREAM MK + Leadership is destined to become a world leader in leadership training and development. I am learning how to monetize living my perfect day every day.

There is so much joy and happiness in my life. The extraordinary has become the ordinary.

I am not one hundred percent sure what will happen next. But here's what I know for sure: the universe has my back. I am going to be just fine.

What I learned at an even deeper level during these turbulent times is that it's really important to know myself better than anyone else does. This includes an ever-higher level of awareness, attention and intention... constant searching and never giving up.

I also need to know my big "Why". What's my personal vision; what's my purpose in life? If I don't know this, I could be living somebody else's dream.

It's also important to make a plan... and a plan B, and a plan C. There is comfort in knowing I have options. I need to follow the plan yet have enough flexibility to let in new opportunities.

I also appreciate the importance of commitment. Driving down the middle of the road is a dangerous place to be. I need to pick a lane and go for it.

Finally, I need go measure what matters. What gets measured gets done. Combined with self awareness, observing your actions, behaviors and habits gives me great insight into my beliefs and values.

I would like to close this chapter with a quote from spiritual leader Mahatma Gandhi:

"Your beliefs become your thoughts, your thoughts become your words, your words become your actions, your actions become your habits, your habits become your values, your values become your destiny."

About the Author
Robin Levesque

Robin Levesque helps organizations co-create positive leadership at every level. His workshops inspire managers and their teams to build healthy employee engagement in the workplace. He also coaches high performers to help them discover their strengths, clarify their personal vision, and develop effective personal learning and resiliency plans.

Results include a healthier workforce, increased productivity, higher employee engagement, better alignment of people and resources, progress on meaningful work, happier employees and customers, and less cynicism, absenteeism, and turnover.

Robin's credentials include 18 years as an industry leader in real estate development, 12 years as a workshop leader, a Master of Arts in Leadership and professional membership in the Project Management Institute, the Canadian Association of Professional Speakers, and the Real Estate Institute of British Columbia.

Robin is the right presenter for your next event if you want your people engaged and embracing the vision of positive leadership and co-creation including personal mastery, team building, and organizational development.

www.robinlevesque.com

Ph: 1-403-458-6611

CHAPTER FIVE

And the Journey Continues

By Yanira Cuellar

Hola! Thank you for coming by.

If you ask me who am I today, and where I am... Who I am is someone who feels incredibly blessed. I have a wonderful family, supportive friends and live in one of the most beautiful places on the planet! I have also discovered a love for dancing and often focus on the music so intently that it feels as if no one is watching.

The question where I am, for me, is a question about where I currently find myself in my spiritual journey. "Am I there yet?" used to be my constant worry and focus. Not too long ago, without directly looking, seeking or pondering, I realized that I felt completely at home in my skin. Sure, I can always stand to lose those stubborn pounds, but even they were a part of me, not something to harass myself for and be ashamed about. I'm still not used to this feeling. Sometimes, it's not there, but most often I find myself feeling at home.

From creating financial systems, implementing payroll structures, running nationwide conferences, training managers, designing budgets, to managing audits of all types, professionally I feel proud of the systems and improvements I have brought to every organization that I worked for.

Where I am today

Today I find myself, again, at the beginning, with the next project, the next client, the next relationship and challenge. I recently realized how much each client reflects where I am in my life—the struggles, lessons and the journey, the triumphs and epiphanies. Some are at the beginning, delving into belief systems and the limits they have placed on themselves. Some clients have done their "work"–meaning they have looked at their issues and what blocks their progress. Even so, they seem to keep dealing with the same or similar challenges and lessons over and over. There is a temptation to judge them and myself for the repeated patterns I see reflected in their lives. Their "why does this keep happening to me?" woes are also mine. I can relate if they wonder, "Why am I working with and/or attracting someone who's angry, overly demanding and critical?" "Why do I continue in a job where my boss lets me know in subtle and not so subtle ways that my work is lacking and I can't be depended upon?" Even with over 35 years' experience, I feel myself listening to the criticism and doubting my skills. The temptation is to fight back, to find something to belittle, to make excuses why I am not. The temptation is to continue the angry and blaming cycle. And it takes every decision not to. It takes a decision to deflect and not take things personally. It takes a decision to believe in myself and know my truth and worth.

I have found certain cycles repeat over and over again. No matter what my achievements have been, there has always been a kernel (it used to be a boulder) of doubt and lack of confidence in my ability to help the next organization, event or project. And I think it is this kernel of doubt that I have projected which has been picked up by people who have their own insecurities and are happy to highlight any deficiencies. It is a power over me that I have allowed others to have. My wish is that when I feel this cycle happening, I untangle, forgive myself for falling into it and bless the other person for bringing the lesson forth.

Breaking the cycle

Did you ever feel not loved by your mother? Did she hug you as if she meant it or did she hold you at a distance and pat your back? Did she ask you at four-years-old to be the "strong one" and not cry or bring shame to the family? Quietly and "strongly", did you watch her walk with your brother to the plaza where they were giving away toys for Christmas? Did she talk to you for 32 years of her anger, feelings of entrapment and resentment? Did she ask you to be "the strong one" when you went to choose her casket and tombstone? Were you surprised, really, that not a cent went to you after she died? Not a mention?

Have you walked into your house ever so slowly, quietly feeling with all your senses to determine if it was safe—or how safe it was to enter? Have you seen the rage in your father's eyes and felt his fist against your face? Violence erupting due to a quick trip to A&W. Have you felt that feeling that you knew it was a matter of time that this would happen to you? After the years of watching him with your mother and brothers—I probably should have been less surprised that it was my turn.

***

The sun was warm, and a breeze filled the air. My son was pulling on a kite string, running on chubby legs. His face so full of joy and his laughter so pure I felt my heart bursting. Our friends followed him to make sure he kept upright and the kite didn't take off with him! I remember the rage and shame that came over me. The realization that by my son's age I had already dealt with abandonment. I already knew then to be the "strong" one and not complain or ask for anything. I already knew that my needs were second to my brother's and the "best" thing for my family was for me to be a "good girl" and to be quiet and preferably unseen. It was in that moment of my son's absolute joy and my abject sadness that I vowed to do what I could do, to make sure he always knew he felt loved and cherished. I vowed to stop the familial cycle and to continue therapy and let go of childhood pain and the horrific memories of abuse.

I started therapy in 1987. My partner at that time kept asking me how I felt and what was wrong. And as much as I tried, all I felt was a hot wave of shame that I felt nothing. That blankness scared me. I wrote in my journal all the time, but when it came to speaking my feelings, I could only express anger. At the time I did not believe in therapy. How does talking about what happened a long time ago change or impact what is happening now?

It took awhile but I realized that I had been repeating patterns of relationships over and over again–repeating cycles where I felt my worth questioned, un-witnessed, unappreciated. No surprise that I have worked with supervisors who were never satisfied, over-demanding and critical and gave little praise.

It took what I call "my hero's journey" to highlight this pattern and to help me stop it or at least minimize it greatly. In retrospect, I appreciate being given the opportunity for the Soul journey, but at the time it was excruciatingly painful. Without planning on it, the Journey gave me a chance at a happier future by coming head to head with my past and the stories of inadequacy, never belonging, and never being good enough.

Shortly before immigrating to Canada, I accepted a position with a US national private foundation. The director hired me to help the department with project management and to assist in creating systems for national convenings. It was a wonderful opportunity for me to use my extensive financial and management skills (my previous most recent position was Finance & Admin Director at Seattle's Pike Place Market) and to be part of a newly created department whose mission was improving the lives of youth in foster care. I was excited for new challenges and the opportunity to help youth and families.

You are not defined by your position but by who you are

In my new job, my direct supervisor had expected an administrative assistant while I had been hired for project management. I still do not understand how that mistake was made since I did not have the skills of an administrative assistant. Over the years, I had relied on the expertise of administrative assistants and appreciated their skill in dealing with numerous details. In my first day of work I was asked to type envelopes and labels. I had to ask the help of a kind administrative assistant who taught me about formatting!

The department manager looked at my resume and commented: "You could be running this department. You could be doing my job." I was quick to tell her that I wanted to expand my project management skills, and that I did not want her job. I had had enough of being responsible for organizations and staff and budgets. I wanted to use my experience to help her department succeed. I think all she heard was that I was not her administrative assistant. Since she could not undo my hiring and complain to the director, the only thing left was to shun me. I was left out off the "family" structure she had set up within the department where she was the "mom," and there were "twins", "cousins", and "aunties." She made it known to me that I was there to "support" her department staff and my opinion and experience were irrelevant. Twenty-five years of accounting, management, and project management were not welcomed. I was emotionally abandoned and physically shunned.

Around that time, I came upon this statement, "You are not defined by your position, but by who you are." Without the title of director, manager, supervisor, or even project manager, who was I? And how was I to affect change in an organization without a title?

After the first conference, I was harshly criticized for not doing my job. Unfortunately, no one had told me what that job was: arrive early, make copies, and get the coffee going?

The conference after that, the organizer left for vacation without leaving details of those invited and to be supported by the organization or the contract with the hotel and conference site. Once again, I was called in and criticized for the job I had done. When I presented my points, I was dismissed and told I was not the educator and that I didn't understand the foster care system. I was told that I should have anticipated what needed to be done and especially known how participants were going to get back to the airport.

One of my biggest contributions was done anonymously. I heard the "twins", "mom" and "aunties" celebrating a large funding by the board for an online training program to address issues of racism in the foster care system. One caveat by the board was that the project had to be completed by the end of the year. That meant they had about 4 months to deliver a project that hadn't been scoped out in any detail. It would involve programmers, writers, photographers, social workers, youth, and foster families. In my experience the department couldn't succeed in that time frame so I took my concerns to a newly created department. They were able to work with the department and executive board to produce a successful project that went live—3 years later.

***

A few months after I started the position, I had just gotten up from the dentist chair and completely froze from shooting and excruciating pain coursing through my body. I could hardly breathe and I couldn't move without jolts of pain. The dentist called the ambulance while I took short breaths. The ambulance trip seemed to take a long time as each bump in the road brought searing pain throughout my body. I felt that I had to focus not to pass out. I was at the ER for almost three hours completely knocked out by sedatives that forced my back to stop spasming.

It was near my 50th birthday and when I returned back to the office the day after my ER episode, I was given a gift and birthday card. Ten years later, I remember them well. The card said, "When you get everyone to sign this card, pigs will fly." The gift was a very tight choker necklace. Maybe it was just a coincidence but at the time it did not feel that way.

Slowly and with the help of good therapist, I began to see that I had stepped into their criticisms and rejections and I had made it all about me. Yes, the ridicule and meanness had been directed at me but it wasn't about me. I believe it was about the other's insecurities and her staff's rally to protect her. I realized I had given the group the power to hurt me.

The stress affected me physically to the point where I had frequent fainting spells, which my acupuncturist attributed to extreme stress on the pancreas. At one point she said that I needed to make an immediate change to my job or it was going to kill me. Unfortunately, with the Landed Immigration application in process I didn't think it was wise to move to another job. I felt trapped.

Trauma related therapy such as Eye Movement Desensitization and Reprocessing, Cognitive Behavioral Therapy, and Emotional Freedom Technique helped tremendously. One of the biggest gifts of the Journey was realizing first-hand the direct correlation between emotional health and physical health. As I healed emotionally, my body became stronger.

I was reminded that we are beings made of energy and we react positively or negatively to energy that we transmit and receive. Therefore, I realized, to change the energy around me I had to change the energy I gave out. If I wanted to be appreciated, I had to first appreciate myself and the focus and integrity that I brought to work.

Every morning I prepared for the job by carrying the memory of my boys' laughter, their giggles, and the joy on their muddy faces as they moved the monster trucks from one construction site to another. I made a list of what I accomplished at work. And I listened to music or meditations on the ferry that I took to commute to work.

The more I prepared myself in this way, the more relaxed I felt. Being more calm started to affect people I worked with. I stopped being defensive, so they stopped rejecting my ideas and suggestions. I was more open and was told I had lighter energy. Without my own barriers, I felt and saw my supervisor relax and her shoulders loosen up. I never did get a familial title like the others in the department, but I did get invited to a cookout!

There was a big push from the division to bring groups together to improve the foster care system by having professionals, families and youth share information and experiences. In order to achieve this, meeting places, hotels, and transportation of all kinds had to be coordinated. I was finally able to help the department but in a way that I had not anticipated. I was approved to take a two year professional certificate course on Event Management from The George Washington University. My job consisted of researching different conference sites in cities throughout the U.S. Included in that was to recommend restaurants and hotels. I was picked up in a limousine and taken on tours.

One of my last assignments at the organization was as project manager of a $900,000+ conference bringing together professionals and youth to share tools and knowledge about the issues of ageing out of foster care system. It proved to be the most successful and well organized conference the organization had had.

Shortly after that conference, I received notice that the Landed Immigration application to Canada had been accepted. In the following six months, my partner and I sold our beautiful beloved 4-acre Bainbridge Island home where we had lived for over 20 years and had given birth to two boys. With the help of many dear friends, we caravanned to our new home on the Sunshine Coast, BC where we didn't know anyone. It was a shock to the four of us as our last friends from the caravan turned the corner and we were left standing in the middle of the street wondering what we had done. The boys had left their best friends and we had left a supportive community.

Where my journey has taken me so far

Almost ten years after we left, we became Canadian citizens. The best of coincidence were the three rainbows over the Lions Gate Bridge in North Vancouver as we made our way to the ceremony. Ironically, the affirmation of the decision to move to Canada landed on the day Trump was elected. It has been difficult to watch the changes and polarization that are happening in the U.S. Unfortunately, we had felt this energy growing and we wanted our sons to grow up somewhere with more acceptance and respect.

The journey's ending highlighted for me that I can't stop people from being overly critical, insensitive, or judgmental, but I can stop how I react to it. I can stop jumping into the old story of "not good enough to be loved, appreciated, seen, etc." I can stop taking it personally. I can start being the witness to my own self, start loving my own self, and forgiving the part that I played in my own pain and in bringing pain to others.

5 Tips to choosing success over adversity:

- Don't take it personally
- Forgive yourself first
- Dance as if no one is watching
- Each moment is a new beginning

- Gratitude for all things brings more opportunities for gratitude

Today I know and understand that the learning goes on and on. I used to feel that if I just worked hard enough and figured it out, then I could be happy, successful, loved and transformed. My hard work would pay off and I would arrive, feeling at home. The shedding, the regress, the surprises, "I didn't see it coming times" would no longer happen. But of course, the learning continues. They call it being on your "Path" for a reason.

I've been fortunate to have wise mentors. One of them is Sonia Choquette who I have followed since I picked up the Psychic Pathway workbook. It helped to awaken my intuition and to expand my knowledge of spirituality. Most recently, I completed the "5-weeks to Forgiveness Course" (for me 2 months!). At almost 63, it's time to completely stop blaming my parents on my current choices and reactions. It's time to stop defining my life and success based on their limitations. One of the biggest takeaways for me from the course is to have compassion for myself and for others and to appreciate the learning people have brought to me and to be kind above all.

About the Author
Yanira Cuellar

Yanira Cuellar has over 35 years' experience in financial management, human resources, strategic planning, and policy development for organizations ranging from non-profits to government and commercial enterprises. Her most interesting and challenging position was that of Finance & Administration Director of Pike Place Market. Her most rewarding position was project manager of the "It's My Life" conference dedicated to the issues of aging out of foster care. Her success comes from her ability to detect patterns and find the best route to solutions. She is sensitive to the interconnectedness in organizations which compels her to create and align systems for improvements. She is most happy working in a team environment when there is an open sharing of ideas, respect and fun which has often led to synergistic projects.

Yanira Cuellar Services has been offering bookkeeping, event management, systems improvement and training for the last ten years to artists, retailers, real estate professionals and non-profits located in the Sunshine Coast, British Columbia.

Yanira's education includes a Bachelor of Science in Business Administration, Masters of Business Administration, Professional Certificate in Event Management, Certificate in Facilitation and Leadership Training, and Certificate in Project Management.

Yanira was born in El Salvador and now calls the Sunshine Coast her home. She is the proud mother of two young men. They are hard working, love to be in good physical shape and are genuinely nice people. She has a wonderful co-parent and many friends.

Company Name: Yanira Cuellar Services
City, State: Sunshine Coast, British Columbia
Website: www.yaniracuellar.com
Email: yanira@yaniracuellar.com

CHAPTER SIX

Using the Power of Positive Thought

By Beth Oldfield

Over the last 20 years, I've helped many people reach their fitness goals. I've had a front row seat to see my clients succeed through very challenging circumstances and their dedication and energy has kept me going all this time. I have watched obese students lose weight and reverse disease. I have watched stroke victims shatter expectations and dance! I've motivated through great music, interesting exercises, lots of laughter and love but sometimes people wrongly assume that because I look happy and fit, I must have life all figured out. I can tell you quite pointedly that I've battled feelings of self doubt my entire adult life, struggled with depression and have dealt with crippling grief.

I was able to pull through these difficult times in my life because I knew that people were relying on me for support. This forced me to put one foot in front of the other when I felt like sitting still, and I came to understand the importance of being physically active as a cure. Let me state that again. If you're struggling with negative feelings, exercise will help, and it is often the first thing that most doctors will prescribe. Because of my job, I felt well physically, and this gave me the energy to seek out ways to feel better mentally.

These adversities were difficult to overcome because mental health issues aren't easy to discuss. Realizing that I had to tackle my emotions if I wanted to live my best life, I turned to books and eventually gained the confidence to start talking about my feelings with friends and family. Over the years, I have learned four valuable lessons that keep me on track to this day.

#1 Don't Wait for Perfection!

It's hard for me to discuss my youth with my siblings because I was born ten years after the third child in the family and my experience with my parents was quite different from theirs. I knew my parents to be in poor health for most of my life whereas my brothers and sister had all the adventures, camping and pet owning before I was born. By the time I was a young tween, ready to partake in fun family activities, my parents weren't interested. They had 'been there and done that.' I basically grew up as an only child, within a big family, under different rules and to be fair, with parents who had grown and changed as well.

"Don't be stupid, Beth."

"You can't do that!"

My father said these things to me often throughout my childhood. To this day when I hear the word "stupid" uttered in any context, I cringe. Hearing it over and over had such a devastating effect. It instilled in me a tremendous fear of trying because I figured that if I was unable to do something perfectly, doing it would be stupid. I revered my dad. He had all the answers and he knew best!

I believe that he was trying to protect me from the embarrassment of failure. I have no idea how he was raised as I didn't know my grandparents, but I imagine that he was told very similar things as a kid. I choose to tell myself that my father did the best he could with the tools he had, and I made peace with this long ago.

On his death-bed, when I was 43 years old (he was in his eighties) he told me how proud he was of me and all that I have accomplished, but I was raised thinking I was incapable of many things. I was very shy in school. I was usually the last one picked for teams in gym class. I dropped out of almost everything that my Mom signed me up for, thinking that if I couldn't be the best instantly than continuing was stupid.

The turning point in my life came when I met my husband Peter at 18 years of age. It was my first year of college. He loved all my ideas and believed that I was capable of great things. He has never said, "Beth you can't!" In fact, all Peter ever says is "of course you can!" I literally met my angel that day.

We dated for four years and then got married and in that time, I managed to complete a Bachelor of Arts in English Literature and a Diploma in Education from McGill University. People told us our marriage would fail because we were too young, but we are about to celebrate our 30th wedding anniversary!

Peter designed and made my wedding dress and it was only the second dress he had ever made in his life. Everyone thought we were nuts telling us that weddings are too expensive and that we could not afford to get married. We made all the flowers out of paper (except my bouquet) and my mom made all the food. We were married in the hall of the college where we met, and people still say that ours was their favorite wedding! Was it the stereotypical, perfect wedding? No but it was original and a true reflection of us.

Peter has shown me that we are capable of anything that we set our minds to and the proof is in the pudding, so to speak, or in the house. We designed and built our first house with our own hands in 1993, six months after our first child was born.

We had just enough money to buy the land and knew that this was the only way we were going to be able to afford a house. And then in 2001, we built another house three time the size of the first, right next door, because we had two more children! By the way, we didn't do any of the above perfectly. We moved into the second framed, unfinished house with three babies and basically camped in a wooden tent for the summer, but we did it. And my kids have wonderful stories to carry with them for a lifetime.

The biggest lesson that I can share with you is to not wait until things in your life are lined up perfectly to get started. Doing it our way, which was messy and bizarre to most people who knew us, made the experience uniquely our own and we are very proud of all we have done both together and separately.

Most people would be surprised to find out that I love to write and one of my goals was to publish a book. After doing my research I learned that it's hard to get publishers to consider your work unless you have an online following. So, I did something totally nuts. I started my own blog which I had absolutely no idea how to do! I bought a book and followed the step by step advice and within a week it was live. Was it perfect? NO. Did it meet my expectations? Yes. It allowed me to communicate with my students. I wrote daily blog posts for over a year as a way of communicating with them outside of the gym. I now write a weekly blog on my website and I get approximately 200 page views a day. Not bad for a girl with low self esteem!

Writing weekly posts gave me the confidence to write the manuscript for a fitness book. It took close to two years to write and then I hired a photographer to take 100+ photos of the exercises. There was no turning back now, but I was still afraid. I was thinking, "What did I know?" "I am not the best fitness trainer!" "Who's going to want to read what I have to say?" "I am no one."

And then a good friend of mine died from cancer. She was only a few years older than me.

I came to realize in a very real way, that life is short, and we need to get things done before it is too late.

All I had to do was find a publisher. I spoke with two companies that do self publishing and, in the end, I went with Prominence Publishing. I didn't want to wait any longer. I wanted to make this dream a reality. Fundamental Fitness After Fifty – Three at Home Fitness Programs to Keep You Functionally Fit for Life came out in March of 2018. A dream comes true!

All I have accomplished thus far has happened because I stopped trying to be perfect, waiting for the perfect time or the perfect amount of money and instead got on with the business of living. We don't know how much time we have so the time is now. Go for it and don't let anything stand in the way of your dreams.

#2 Use the Power of Positive Thought

If you told me that one day, I would find myself driving 180km/hr down a dark, country highway at 2:00 am on wintry morning with tears blurring my vision, I would have called you insane. If you told me that my dangerous behavior would be the result of having lost my mother suddenly to a disease that she never told me she had, I would laugh in your face. If you told me that I would miss saying good-bye to her by mere minutes because I was too lazy, I would call you a liar and tell you that you don't know me, that you don't know how devoted a daughter I was to my mother. I wish that none of the above had ever happened, but it did on March 28th, 2007 and it was the beginning of one of the darkest periods of my life.

My story is one of hope despite the beginning of that difficult time. I had just turned 40 on March 8th. I had three kids, 14, 12 and 10 years of age of whom I was very proud. I had just purchased my first brand new car, as my midlife crisis present. I loved my job as a fitness instructor and I was 18 years married to my best friend, Peter. Everything was going along swimmingly, until Mom called and told me she was feeling unwell and had fallen.

I had no idea that Mom would end up in emergency room that night, clinging to life. Post-mortem, the emergency physician told me that it was one of the worst cases of renal failure that he had ever seen and that my mother should have been on dialysis at least three months beforehand. I believe that she knew that she was very ill, but she didn't want to be a burden to myself or my wheelchair bound dad, so she arranged her exit from this world without consulting any of her family.

In retrospect, her plan was brilliant. She wanted to control how she died, and she managed to do this on her terms. As painful as it was to the family left behind, my mother, who loved Frank Sinatra, lived and died "her way."

Thankfully, I survived that dangerous car ride, but my life changed drastically that evening. Not only was I now without my Mother, my biggest fan, but I had become the primary caregiver to my dad who was less than nice. I had replaced his wife in a sense, and he was quite rude to her when she was alive. Suddenly, I was being spoken to like I was that stupid little girl again. I fell into despair. I had three teenagers, three jobs and at the end of every day I had to visit a mean old man who made me feel like I was not good enough. Often, I would drive home in tears, wishing I could do more to help his situation. I knew that he was suffering so I kept the pain in, and it slowly began to eat away at my heart.

After a year of wondering if I would ever feel happy again, I knew I had to seek help and I found The Secret. Rhonda Byrne and the contributing authors taught me the tools of positive thought.

> *"If you are feeling bad, it is because you are thinking thoughts that are making you feel bad."*
> *–Lisa Nichols.*

This sounds quite logical and sensible, but it hit me like a brick. I was so stuck on thinking about how miserable my life had become that I had stopped looking at its greatness.

> *"Nothing can come into your experience unless you summon it with persistent thoughts."*
> *–Dr. Joe Vitale.*

Well, I knew that I didn't want to feel unhappy anymore, so I had to stop focusing on that and switch up my thoughts. I was desperate to change my life, and this seemed like a painless way to bring about positive change, so I wrote custom mantras (statements repeated frequently) to try to reverse my negative thought patterns and hopefully improve my life. People joke about the Secret bringing them cars or bicycles. I just wanted to stop crying. I wanted the ache in my heart to go away.

Bob Proctor suggests that we start with yelling the following to the universe, "Life is so easy! Life is so good! All good things come to me!"

His words became the basis for my first mantra, the one that I still recite today if I begin to feel despair coming on. "Life is good. Life is easy. All good things are coming to me."

I literally repeat this statement over and over again until I feel myself relax and find myself in a space of gratitude. I then give thanks for the simple things that are going right. For example, the fact that my car is working that day or that the sun is shining or that I have a delicious lunch planned that afternoon. This mantra helped me so much that I created four others that revolve around the other worries that hijack my thoughts occasionally: my health and money concerns.

Mantras and the power of positive thought transformed my life in short order. I recommend writing your own and you will find that with regular use, you can overcome negative emotions which will help you on your journey to achieving your goals.

#3 You will be whatever you believe

"You're not strong enough!"

To be fair, my boss at the time didn't say these words exactly that way but that is what I heard. I had just completed my Fitness Instructor certification and I had asked for a night class at the YMCA that I was helping to run during the day, and he said, "No, I need strong teachers at night."

I was devastated. I was so full of hope and energy about bringing new fitness moves to our friends at the gym, people I knew and had exercised with for years. But in his eyes, I was not strong enough. He didn't even give me a chance to prove myself.

The old me, the low self esteem little girl, would have agreed and gone away peacefully but the new me took in those words and used them to motivate me to become the strongest, best trainer I could possibly be. I studied harder, practiced longer and promised myself that I would prove him wrong.

Shawna, the woman who taught me how to teach, ended up giving me my first job at different club. She called me about half way through the 12-week session to tell me how she thought I was doing. She told me that she had a big problem!

"Your class is so much in demand that I have had to start a waiting list and now I have to open a second class in order to accommodate all of the new students!" Those words are one of the highlights of my career.

Instead of giving up, I used that initial disappointment to fuel my quest to be the best! I chose to believe that I could be an effective, strong leader and it has worked. I continue to lead people on their fitness journey at that same club 20 years later. I went from teaching one class to ten and these years have been incredibly rewarding.

Don't Become the Disease

The first time that we get labelled with a disease, time stops.

"What do you mean? I'm doing everything right. I eat right, I exercise, I don't smoke. This can't be true!"

When it happened to me it was a slow, painful process.

In my mid forties I discovered two tiny spots on the back of my legs as if I had been bitten by a mosquito but after weeks, they were persistently itchy and by then more spots had appeared on my both of knees, both of my ankles and both of my elbows. It took close to two years of being told I was allergic to all manner of things for a friend who is also a dermatologist to tell me to try taking gluten out of my diet. Well, the difference was night and day.

Dermatitis Herpetiformis is only hard to live with if you get exposed to gluten. I was happy to finally figure out what was wrong, but I grew quite depressed as I couldn't eat or socialize normally. I really felt like I had lost my identity as a great cook and provider for my family. The food I tried to make in the beginning was horrible. I went from being an amazing chef to someone who was afraid to eat.

I sank into despair and stopped socializing for quite awhile. I felt isolated and alone. I lost ten pounds quite quickly. I became the disease and believed that my life was irreparably altered.

My mantra, "Life is good. Life is easy. I am thankful for my healing and I am perfectly healthy" helped me to gain perspective on my condition.

I have met new people who share my allergy to gluten. I am happy to report that I have become an excellent cook and baker once again and I have regained the weight and then some unfortunately!

We may get sick, but we do not have to become the condition. I had to learn to treat DH as just something that I had, not who I was. I was still a fun-loving social woman, I just had to find new ways to enjoy the company of my friends and family. I reclaimed my life by finding a way to be fully me, gluten free.

I have watched my students battle arthritis, cancer, diabetes, high blood pressure and heart disease and I have learned by watching them that we cannot turn inward and try to go it alone. Instead we must turn outward and ask for help.

Therein lies the key to overcoming adversity. Ask questions, listen to the answers and you will redefine who you are in the process. I had to believe that I was fine and healthy in order to get back to my happy self.

I am stronger and healthier without gluten in my diet. I feel better at 51 than I did in my thirties. I'm now able to offer help and hope to others who suffer from this condition. I believe that everything that occurs in our lives places us right where we are supposed to be, so instead of drowning in despair over what has changed, try to look at the opportunities for growth that lie within.

#4 Change Your Environment

It is very easy to fall into the trap of thinking that we are the first ones to feel despair or sadness and that no one else could possibly know what we are going through.

Part of my healing took place when I started to take a different route to work. I decided that I wanted to feel as though I was on vacation every day. I left extra early and it literally changed my life.

Instead of rushing through traffic, worrying about my job, I would detour down to the lakeshore road and while on that slow journey, I would repeat my mantras and focus on positive thoughts.

I have longed to live in one of these little lakeshore towns since Peter and I first met. I decided to play a game with myself and pretend that we owned one these cute homes. Instead of thinking that I was not good enough, I turned my feelings around and gave thanks for the opportunity to be right there at that moment, enjoying the view. I would arrive at work more relaxed and grateful for life.

And then something magical happened.

A friend of mine who has done various forms of art therapy invited me to one of her groups. The workshop was held each week, in a lovely home on the lakeshore, the very area that I would pass each day on my way to work. Instead of just admiring from afar, I had the chance to see these homes from the inside!

Now I am now lucky to call many of those women living along the lakeshore road among my closest friends. I thought I wasn't good enough to be among people who could afford to live in such a place, and now after years of socializing, I see that we are all just the same, with the same problems and emotions, worries and concerns.

After a year of doing art together, my friends on the lakeshore began what is called a Women's Circle. Twice per month we meet, sit in a circle and listen to each other speak from the heart. No one makes comments or suggestions. We get a chance to give voice to the thoughts in our head that can literally drive us mad if they never get out! We cry, and we laugh but we never interrupt the speaker and we are not allowed to address anyone who has spoken previously. It is simply a safe space to speak our minds and emotions.

This process of listening magically shows us our commonalities. By the end of each circle we have heard our own voice in the voices of others, and we realize that we are not alone. Once more, I have found that by the time I have completely spoken my ideas, and actively listened to the group, I usually end up resolving my issues. I always walk away feeling better. Listening circles are truly magical. I hope that you can find one in your area or start one with your own friends.

My Lessons:

Don't wait for things to be perfect to start living because we don't know how much time we have on this earth to complete our goals.

You are stronger than you realize. Use positive thinking and personalized mantras to keep you on track toward achieving your dreams.

You will be whatever you believe yourself to be, so choose wisely and speak about yourself in only positive ways.

Change your environment and, in the process, you will find like-minded people who can help you along your journey.

Remember that diamonds are formed under extreme pressure. I believe that adversity helps us to carve our true selves out of the family mold. We have inherited much from past generations, but we need to step forward, be ourselves and claim this time as our chance to shine.

Good luck!

About the Author
Beth Oldfield

Beth Oldfield has been teaching fitness for 20 years in Pointe-Claire, Quebec. Participants ranging in age from 20 to 85 years young embrace her enthusiasm and energy by filling her classes to capacity. Beth's mission is to educate and motivate her students to be the best that they can be in body, mind and spirit. Her specialties include Aerobics, Step, Muscle Conditioning, Yoga, Line Dance and Essentrics.

Beth currently commutes to work from the country where she has been living for 25 years with her husband Peter. Together they have designed and built two homes with their own hands and raised three beautiful children who are now successful adults. When she is not teaching, reading or writing short stories and updating her weekly fitness blog at betholdfield.ca, she is cooking delicious gluten free food.

Beth's designations include:

- Bachelor of Arts, Diploma in Education – McGill University

- Best-Selling Author of Fundamental Fitness After Fifty: Three At Home Fitness Programs to Keep You Functionally Fit For Life

- Fitness Instructor Specialist

- Personal Training Specialist

- Older Adult Specialist – Canfitpro

Connect with Beth Oldfield at http://www.betholdfield.ca

CHAPTER SEVEN

Source Energy

Dr. Lesya Anna

"Your entire universe is in your mind and nowhere else. To expand the universe, expand your mind"
– Deepak Chopra

I'm guessing this is probably not the first time you've heard of the "law of attraction" or "manifesting" through "visualization". The first thing I want to mention is that if you've failed at using these techniques, or manifesting consistently was a "hit and miss" experience, or you manifested parking spots but not that dream house, or dream spouse, it's not your fault. There's a lot of information out there and it can be confusing. Many times, that information overload keeps you from success. It's okay.

If you've been concerned in the past that you just can't succeed with this "woo woo talk", I want to put those fears to rest. You can do this. You just need the right person to explain it to you.

Most of the world works on believing "what is". They tell you to 'get real' and stop believing in the spiritual stuff, to work harder, say the right thing and get your mate, start taking this chemical drug, or buy this shiny trinket, and you will feel better. And because it gives you that temporary hit of dopamine, it does feel better. For a moment. But your life is still the same, the clutter and disappointment build and you have less money and feel deflated because nothing has really changed. When you find yourself at the same place you were a year ago, and you're ready to give up—don't.

If you've ever thought that the people with the 'real money' really want you to fail, you're probably right. They don't benefit from you succeeding. They benefit from keeping you in debt, depressed, anxious and in need. The difference with me is I truly want to see you living the life of your dreams. So much so, I put my house up to help produce a movie that helps you understand, from a quantum science perspective, how to actually manifest the life you dream of.

My goal for this chapter is for those who have tried all sorts of "laws of attraction" or other manifesting techniques that just left you feeling frustrated and deflated and believing that you are a victim of a cruel world that is stacked against you, to instead feel consistently connected to the universal Source Energy that can and does respond to the desires of your heart. It's a usable method of quantum physics.

I want to show you how you can build this incredible Source Energy up in your body-mind and become so at one with it, that your manifesting abilities become second nature. It will feel like everything magical is showing up just for you. Your manifesting and synchronicity skills will accelerate rapidly, your 'luck' will happen at will, and your stress will melt away. This is the ONLY method I teach because it works. Stress melts away, depression lifts and opportunities for greater health and wealth arise.

My name is Dr. Lesya Anna Adehl. After life as a chiropractor, acupuncturist & integrative nutritionist, I became obsessed with the mind-body connection and how the brain affects our lives. When my marriage failed, depression set in. My parents both passed away far too young, and I found myself in a position where my house was about to be repossessed.

***

What I learned was amazing and powerful, but I was still making mistakes and living as if I could actually control the outside world with force instead of Divine power. But the universe, God, or Source Energy always gives us opportunities to awaken and see what power lies just on the other side of faith & intention.

I'm going to share with you the most dramatic story I had with this energy. Later, I will share more stories, but I really want to share with you how much this energy can do for you.

Several years ago, I was on a call with my banker as my husband and I were unsuccessful at selling our home, yet we had already bought a second home to downsize (we were separating, which was devastating enough!) I had thought we were going to have a bridge loan to get us through the sale process. But we misunderstood and the banker informed us that without a signed sale document, we owed the bank $1.3 Million and it was due in 5 days! Essentially, we had to either find a buyer for our home (which was not looking good) or come up with the funds or we would be bankrupt and our homes would be repossessed. We had 5 days. Two of which were a weekend! The level of fear was incredibly deep. The point of crisis was never bigger in my life.

In this moment, I knew that the universe made me dig deep into all I had learned about manifesting and energy, and stop the downward spiral into the anger, guilt, shame and fear. There was no time for that.

I could have easily spiraled into seeing my whole life as a failure. My marriage was broken and I was feeling my life was a lie and now it looked like I would lose my house as well. But the Source Energy works in mysterious and gracious ways, and if we believe one thing, we can overcome anything. I will tell you what that one thing is a little later.

This time, there was no time for me to think. I did not have parents to save me. I had a daughter to care for. I had given up being a doctor so that I could be present and raise her without nannies or daycares. Somewhere along those years, I had forgotten who I was, and was living fully from forcing things to happen, rather than in the energy of flow and miracles. I was pushing every day to make things happen the way I thought they should, and everything was a struggle and often not very positive.

Now, this moment was a lesson and lessons are gifted to us for growth. Even though, at the time, it did not feel that way at all!

There was extremely limited time to come up with. $1.3 Million dollars and despite the irrationality of it being a possibility, I refused to listen. What some people will tell you is Impossible, is only an opinion.

Instinctively, I began to incorporate everything I had learned up to that point. I pulled from the time I spent in the jungles of Brazil and Indonesia studying with energy masters, the time I studied with various medical, chiropractic, acupuncture doctors and other energy workers. I had studied yogic principles and Zen mind laws. And thank God, the time I spent learning real estate, investing & creating a roster of incredible contacts with my parents! I was so lucky to have had them.

Over the course of 2 decades, I had spent close to $200,000 researching how health is truly manifested but I really didn't apply it to wealth or relationships. Instead, I continued to allow myself to be surrounded by my fears, doubts and trying to make things happen with will power. Clearly, it was not working. Now, the chips were all in and I had to go back to the only source that would save me: I connected to my inner power (and I show people exactly how later in the chapter) and then, I connected to the Source Energy, or Goddess, the One Divine, the energy that has been felt and experienced and taught by great masters from around the globe for over 5000 years.

It's not that hard actually, but it does take consistent practice. It is a living energy and desires a connection as much as you do. But it does not require mountains of guilt or shame for who you are (Catholic Church remnants!)

"If we interpret the ideas of quantum physics liberally and with a generous dose of imagination, we can begin to understand that for each possible outcome many other probability realities can occur – perhaps even some things that would be considered impossible within the context of our mutually assured construction of reality."

– Richard Bartlett, DC, ND

It didn't take long to 'hear' my answer, because I had trained through yoga & meditation for so long prior to this.

You see, Source Energy works through people and action!

And then, I "heard" that inner voice tell me who to call. You may get answers through that inner voice we call intuition through seeing signs, meeting just the right person, hearing a song on the radio, or receiving a call or text that comes to show you the way. Trust that you have aligned with the right energy because you have made that a parameter of your journey.

The first person I called was a mortgage broker I had worked with in the past, but that I had not thought of for many years. Incredibly, he shared that he had just finished a call with a gentleman who had just sold his home and was looking to put $1.1 Million dollars somewhere to earn some interest. He said he would get back to me to confirm if this opportunity was still available. What?! That simply blew me away. But even if it worked out, I would still be $200 thousand short.

I sat and waited for him to call me back, and focused deeply on my breath and the KNOWING & BELIEVING that the universe loves me. Finally, I called an old friend, who also, incredibly, shared that he had just sold his home, and would gladly help me with a $200,000 loan to tide me over until I was able to sell my home. Since I already had a mortgage and now a second one from a private investor, this third loan would be without any collateral.

It was a true miracle.

From facing bankruptcy to two phone calls later, I had enough to cover my debt to the bank. By Monday afternoon, I was signing papers to cover the loans. I am deeply grateful for the experience of knowing the power of real estate + strong connections.

I share this story with you, not to impress you, but to bless you with the tools you need to build resilience, to harness an invisible power, truly use prayer to ask for help and then know how to listen for the right answer.

Here is the process I used

Yes, I am sharing it openly. Know that this system is a developed muscle that grows stronger with use and exponentially improves when you work it with others. I invite you join our FB group and join the expansion into the energy field with us there and really get your manifesting muscle built up!

1. Command your mind. Mentally, physically and vocally command the matrix to STOP. Training your mind is happening every day, every moment by

the soup matrix. So if you want to heal the mind, you must train it first to STOP.

2. Breathe. You must be in a state of relaxation as the mind body works its creative best when in the brain is in an alpha state. This will also get better with time and will begin to happen at will because you have spent the time training your mind.

3. Get Present. Notice what you Notice. Just notice what is. You MUST start from a clear perspective of where you are, in space. NOTICE the table, the chair, the room. Feel the chair support you and feel how Source Energy is supporting you through that chair or floor. As Albert Einstein once said, the fundamental choice becomes whether the universe is a friendly place or not.

4. Bring in the Light. Envelop your body, home and loved ones in protective light energy.

5. Ground to the earth. This is your supportive anchor. You do not need to know the HOW right away. Faith first.

6. Visualize and feel your desired outcome. All other ideas must not be allowed in, not even for a moment. This takes practice and requires discipline. It may also mean releasing some friendships or relations that do not serve you. But you can do it. Get 100% Focused.

7. Bring in more light and begin to clear away limiting beliefs or attachments. There is an incredibly powerful way to do that, which I explain on my Facebook page. Don't miss this one.

8. Center your energy in your heart, the place of purest potential. Dropping into your heart allows you to collapse the wave of reality, because there is no mind to distract it.

9. Expand your energy into space. This is the true place of creation is actually in the SPACE. BOOM!

10. Collapse the energy wave from the reality of where you are to the reality of where you want to be. I explain an incredibly potent time collapsing method so your brain mirrors what you DESIRE rather than what you worry about. I know you get this one.

11. Believe in the higher power of guides (Jesus, Mary, Buddah, Angels) and their desire to help you. Set it up so only the good guides & entities come.

12. Declare & Ask the Energy aka PRAYER: like a ROYAL. Imagine the Royal Throne and get back up on it and never fall off again!

Declaration: I refuse to believe this is all there is for me in this vast universe! "Thou shalt not forsake us". We are promised in every sacred text on the planet that God loves us yet we behave as if that's not true. Change that belief FOR-EV-Ah!

ASK: What would an infinite being of pure potential energy DO, SEE AND FEEL ?

13. Then LET IT BREATHE. If you stand over it and block the sun, give it too much rain and tug at it all the time, you will kill it. Let it breathe. Send it

love. Trust that the universe is a friendly, expanding and helpful place. There is a power greater than you. It is all around us and goes in every direction. It works as an electromagnetic force that you can experience but you cannot see. Trust that it is your intention that directs it.

I'm sorry to say this is not a get rich quick process. Rather, it is a get happy quick and learn to grow your dreams. I started life on humble ground, with my parents working for everything they provided for us. I had no special talents. These things happened because of the years of saving, building relationships and cultivating my mindset to invest in myself and my future. I do not promise instant anything. I promise that if you learn these methods and incorporate them and then take action to learn what you want to do in life with passion, you will find your own success.

My conditions: This is NOT for you if you want to use it for purely selfish purposes. Notice, I said "purely" selfish. It's ok to treat yourself and be kind and generous with yourself, but it is imperative to share & be kind to others and wish well on all humanity. Humanity thrives on co-operation and selfless giving. Do your share in giving selflessly as well as your own and we all become happier.

I tell you this story, with full humility. I took the proceeds from that miracle and I went on to create a full length feature documentary about this powerful knowledge, called The Connected Universe, which you can download here (limited quantities): www.lesyaanna.com and there we go deep into understanding the science & quantum physics of this energy field.

Manifesting my $1.3 Million Dollar Miracle was pretty fast for me as I had practiced a lot prior to this point. I do not promise similar results. Results will vary based on your own choices and actions which I cannot control. Also, you are responsible to the relationships you choose to build, especially the one you have with yourself.

My goal is to help millions of people experience this energy and learn to play with it and have greater opportunities to help themselves gain greater health, greater opportunities for wealth and fantastic relationships that build memories and lasting love. Let me tell you that it is not a magic pill, it is a method of being and doing that makes everything easier and faster and way more fun.

You see, we all have many courses and products that we have bought to find health, wealth or success. And we have started them and failed, we have gotten stuck again and again and again.

This is a system that is simple, backed by science and downright works.

It's not just the Law of Attraction, it is the Quantum Law of Oneness & Divine Intention. Your work is to build clarity of vision, heart of courage and creative possibilities. You will be amazed at what the universe has in store for you! This is not 'woo woo.' It is science + shamanism blended to bring you what works and used by top CEOs and celebrities, doctors and yogis and zen masters from around the globe.

Focused intention is a trained muscle. It comes from a powerful routine to train your mind, body & habits. There is no time. You must act as if this is it. At every moment.

So, for example, when I needed to get Source Energy fast, it was an instinctual process. I immediately took my ego mind that wanted to take me to the conclusion that we were going to be bankrupt instead. This is why I encourage you to start NOW. There is a Zen saying that there are two times in one's life to plant a tree. One was 20 years ago. The other is NOW.

When we try to limit our reality into what we know, we cut off the possibility of what is possible. Be open to things being better than you ever imagined. You can make a rule while in meditation that things will always show up easier and far better than you ever imagined and then notice when they do.

In quantum physics, we learn that the observer directly influences what a molecule or atom appears as. That means, if you show up with an already preconceived notion of what your reality is, then that is what you will see. When you train your heart, brain, the body-mind to be asking THE RIGHT questions, thus allowing for possibility, and give an INTENTION or COMMAND of what you want to experience (so a clear vision of where you want to go), align your energy to the field of Pure Infinite Potential, you open up a portal to changing your 'reality'. How fast you get at collapsing the wave will affect your speed.

Waiting 20 years to make $1,000,000, is only $50,000/year, which is relatively poor.

But I think most would agree that making $1,000,000 in 20 months, makes you rich.

It's the same amount of money, but one leaves you rich, the other poor. The difference? Time.

Make sure you are collapsing the probability wave to make the timeline very short.

***

There is one final and very important part of using the Source Energy. These are not part of the system but are required as amplifiers. Without them, you are using force to find your way through your To Do list rather than Source Energy power.

The gifts of the heart change everything. Once you begin to use them regularly and with intention, you open up the portal to your success even more. Love, in the form of gratitude, forgiveness and compassion are the most powerful ways to live in the heart. And when you drop into the heart, connect it to your mind's intention and your gut's intuition, then you will experience the miracle of consistent synchronicity and events will begin to unfold fast.

Other heart gifts: staying open, playful and grateful for everything that shows up, is also extremely important in this process. If we get into the downward spiral of worry, fear, regret, and/or shame, our energy will follow where you emotionally take it. Make a rule for your reality: my rule is that no matter what or who is in my energy space, I am always receiving and allowing magnificent experiences to uplevel my life. My team is smart & amazing, my family is loving & united and I am a master manifestor. You can set up similar rules for yourself!

Albert Einstein said that imagination is more powerful than knowledge. He also said that knowledge is required to make things happen. So we require both.

To get your desired result, you must train your mind. The mind is brainwashed every day, every minute; as soon as you open your eyes, your mind believes what it "sees" and is told to believe by others. You must train your mind to believe what it does not yet see and begin to test it for yourself. Ray Dalio, in his highly successful book Principles, teaches that every one of us must discern our own truth and then test it out. This is also a Buddhist principle.

I got the miracle I needed and I believe I was given that very powerful experience to share with you how you can have access to this sort of miracle yourself. I call it a miracle but a miracle is only that which we don't understand yet. The thing is, we are now beginning to understand, through quantum science, HOW this energy actually does work. And for those who will listen, the benefits are great indeed.

Shortly after that experience of saving my family from bankruptcy in 5 days, I intuited that I should make a movie about consciousness energy and how we can experience it in a practical way. I had never made a movie in my life or been around movie making at all.

When I shared this thought with my neighbor, a hummingbird came and hovered over my right shoulder for a good 10 Seconds! I can still feel the rapid pulse of the air on my cheek and the hum in my ear and as I mindfully turned to look at the gorgeous bird, I saw the deep royal blue on its throat and bright emerald greens with gold flecks on its body and was in utter awe that this bird was just hovering, entirely for me to get inspired. I took it as a sign that this was indeed to be my next mission.

Soon after, I met the team of people that would later bring together The Connected Universe film, a documentary about a quantum science theory that has gained global recognition in explaining how these waves and particles work and how what you think and believe about yourself really does matter.

> *"Your job is not to seek for love, but to remove all the barriers we have put up to love"*
> *–Rumi*

If you break down why we want anything in life, whether it's money, relationships, or something else, it all breaks down to LOVE. This was an act of true passion and love.

I can teach you the steps in this method, but remember, Source Energy is a living energy that we work with and she works best in community. Know that everything that shows up is a hint, a gift for you to unravel and learn from, even from other people in your life. The good and the bad. You have a beautiful sisterhood and brotherhood of community here waiting for you, so I would love for you to join and bring your dreams and watch them unfold.

Stepping into the life of your dreams will feel uncomfortable at first. You must allow yourself to make the uncomfortable, comfortable. You must allow yourself to go beyond what the matrix world teaches you about how things are, or how they work. Many of you will decide, consciously or subconsciously, that it's too much discomfort, out of your comfort zone to accept as true or possible.

But many of you will read this and tuck it away and go on living lives of hard work and struggle which is what the Matrix tells you every day is 'reality'. You will be convinced by all sorts of sources, usually those closest to you as well, that this is woo woo and a scam. It is up to you to test it out. You are in control of what you choose to experience here. The choice to move forward is always yours.

Although I created a practical method for you to interact with Source Energy so your left brain has something to tap into, your experience will depend on your full body mind heart experiences so the more you connect on FB, in our webinars, and listen to the recordings or watch the movie, the more you will code your energy field with Source Energy and the more the synchronicities will grow.

When you have built your Source Energy muscle, you'll be able to experience incredible synchronicities, know who to connect to next to help you along the way, and get rid of doubt, fear and struggle. Money problems will begin to vanish and your level of happiness and satisfaction will rise exponentially.

When I was first learning all this, I spent over $200,000 studying with the masters, and I ran into a lot of roadblocks. I thought I was failing because I could not consistently stay focused. But after years of research into the science, and learning to understand the quantum energy model, I saw that I did not need to fully understand Source Energy to use it. I developed a system that now I share with you to use. Similar to how you do not need to understand the energy waves my phone uses to work, you can use Source Energy to create miracles in your life as well even if you don't completely understand it yet.

To train the mind, we must have consistent experiences to a new way of being. We start with daily morning meditations, and easy-to-incorporate mind-body exercises to break down the barriers to your own freedom and miracles. As you develop this muscle, you will be amazed how fast and consistently it will work in your life.

You must believe and have faith that you are more than just a brain moving a body around. When you believe that you are a living, infinite spirit and that you are always connected to Source Energy, it's simply your awareness that allows you to direct it.

Remember, you must build the miracle muscle and then it will grow stronger with each experience and each miracle that happens. These experiences will grow with you. And when you share them with others, they will grow faster, stronger and of course, just be more fun too! The universe actually loves to have fun and build beautiful things. Just look at nature and how amazing she is. And look at some of the incredible creations that humanity has created from music to film to architecture to science. Don't limit yourself. Start with small projects to build your miracle muscles up. You will quickly want to apply it to bigger miracles. And you will be ready.

And in case no one told you today, you are enough. I love you.

About the Author
Dr. Lesya Anna

Dr. Lesya Anna knows you have a dream to live better, happier for yourself, your family and even make an impact & change the world. She wants to show you how to make that happen with an amazing amount of ease and fun. From now on, you will have access to information that few people actually get to understand and fewer still will undertake to learn. Most people will just accept what they have in life and go into the negative spiral that the matrix would convince you is 'real'.

To help you keep your mind in the space of free flow and infinite potential, join Dr. Lesya on her Facebook page where she shares a powerful meditation download to help you do this process rapidly and easily. Please Like and Share and help build our community of Quantum Resonance Masters at our Come Alive Life Transformation Academy.

You can find Dr. Lesya at www.lesyaanna.com and at www.comealivetransformation.com where you can download a free e-book and sample meditation and learn how you can begin to practice interacting and calling in Source Energy every day, for absolutely any area of your life.

CHAPTER EIGHT

Losing and Gaining Control

By Izabela Adams

It was a cold, mid-November morning as I sat on the balcony of my newly rented apartment, snuggled in a blanket with a coffee in my hand. Thousands of thoughts were passing through my mind and I was trying to organize them like a well-functioning computer with a very complex operating system. Or so I hoped.... You see, the problem is that my operating system doesn't always work that way. The files are not in orderly, well-marked folders. The best way to describe my mind is chaos– thoughts everywhere, and hard to catch and hold on to them. My brain likes to skip beats often and there is nothing I can do about it.

I take a deep breath, and then another and another, thinking, That's the easiest thing I did this morning. Breathing. Just breathing. I didn't have to think about it, it was so easy. If you only knew. Just a few weeks earlier I took breathing for granted, until I was rushed to ICU because my airway was closing. After that traumatic experience, I will no longer take for granted the gift of breath.

As I slowly inhaled and exhaled, noticing the gorgeous view of the forest that I am lucky to have, I smelled beautiful autumn in the air. And oh, the colors of those leaves! I noticed, perhaps for the first time, how beautiful it is outside. I am on the go so much, sometimes I forgot to look around me and appreciate the beauty of the world. It is nature in its purity. The smell in the air and those colors of the trees very much reminded me of my home country of Poland. With fascination and excitement, in seconds I was "back home" where I grew up; being a kid who would not sit on the chair on a first-floor balcony but would be climbing the trees fearlessly. I smiled, and like a lightning strike, in a second, maybe two, my whole life flashed in front of my eyes. I felt tears streaming down my face. So many years had passed, and so many life events lead me to this very moment.

My name is Izabela Adams, and this is my story.

How I've learned to notice myself

Over the years I've heard that your early childhood is what shapes you. My personal opinion is that 'yes', it gives us the base, but throughout our entire life we can keep changing and re-shaping our life, if we are open to it.

I was born and raised in Legnica, Poland at a time when communism ruled the country. Propaganda, poverty, thievery and lies were fed to us as a nation for many years. My city was called "the second Moscow" because, for years, Russia treated Poland as their second home, and we were forced to learn the Russian language from early childhood. But we learned to view our "protective neighbors" as the enemy. Often, when people ask, 'What was it like growing up in Poland?' I simply reply, "Everyday was like black Friday because there was absolutely nothing in the stores, unless there was a delivery, which was rare." We lined up for miles to buy a chicken for Sunday dinner, just to find out at times that it was all sold out. As a child, I remember people shouting and get into physical altercations. It was like that with almost everything. But I think the most successful hunting day was when there was a delivery of toilet paper. I know it might sound silly, but to us it meant no newspaper in the bathroom! For dessert, we would have raw sugar with egg yolk or bread sprinkled with sugar. A banana was a luxury we enjoyed only once or twice a year. 'Til this day I recall how we could eat one banana for hours, treating like it was a lollipop, so we could remember the taste until the next time. I grew up in a tiny one-bedroom apartment with my younger sister and both parents. Physical discipline was a typical punishment. My mom was a stay-at-home mom and I've always said that she stayed home because she needed to come up with physical punishments; she was pretty creative.

There was no such thing as money given to us. I knew that if I wanted a piece of chocolate, I would have to collect milk, beer or other bottles by scrounging on the streets. I didn't care to dig through the trash, but my creativity to make some pocket money was always brewing.

I was bullied for a long time when I was young because I was a good student and interested in music, which other kids thought was weird, so they didn't like me. I had to change schools to escape. When I was 11 years old, I got punched really hard in the face. That punch cost me 13 medical procedures and surgeries with last one just 5 years ago... it was like a ticking bomb.

We always knew that there was a dreamland far, far away called the USA, but no one was allowed to talk about it. As a matter a fact, anything to do with government we had to whisper; my father used to say, "The walls have ears."

Leaving your life like that, and not knowing any better, makes you not question your home, your classmates, teachers, nation or country in general.

I've always dreamed big. I was convinced that I would travel the world and would visit the long-forbidden America! I made sure that my focus stayed on the target and my choices, even at a young age, would count towards making my dreams come true!

I remember in 8th grade, my Physics teacher asked everyone what we wanted to be when we grew up. When it was my turn, I said that I wanted to be a musician who travels around the world and shares her music with people from other cultures. The teacher mocked me front of the entire class. She laughed at me and said, cruelly, "You are going to be a 'no-body.'" Those words are with me to this day, for many reasons, but mostly because at that time I knew they could either make or break me. Well, I was on a mission! While attending musical high school, I came to realize that I could use my skills (in music and dance) to earn some money. I started to teach piano lessons, and I set up and conducted large choirs. I also organized a kids' dance group with 50 members. In order to do this, I had to apply for a license, which I successfully obtained. Then I choreographed all the dance pieces and took the group on the road to successfully compete in national events. I did all of this while still in high school, which was unheard of at that time. Upon my graduation from high school, I was approached by a principal from a brand-new middle school (the largest one in my city at that time) to come and not only teach, but also write a brand-new curriculum for the entire music department. I became a lead teacher at the age of 19. I went to college on the weekends while working 3 jobs during the week. One day, I got that knock on my door with an offer to travel and play music while seeing the world. My hard work had paid off. People had heard about my skills and work ethic and wanted to work with me. I was only 21 years old.

My travels took me all around the world, including the Middle East. I worked in Dubai, Bahrain, and Abu Dhabi. I think those 4 years in the Middle East were the biggest test of my strength and ability to adopt not only to critical situations but also patiently plan and find the best solutions to get out of them.

At one point, I was kept captive, against my will, for 3 months. My room was locked from the outside and I was only allowed to leave my room with the security staff. I couldn't leave the country, as my passport and visa were taken away from me, and I had no family or anyone close who could have helped me. I could only count on myself and on my perseverance.... I remember like it was yesterday, the look on my parents' faces when they saw me de-boarding the airplane. They thought they would never see me again.

I lasted in Poland for only a few months. I had to get back on the road, I had to get my suitcases pack and see the world, settling was not an option. Next stop - "the dream-land", United States!

Believing in me

I came to the US as an Au Pair in 1998 not knowing much English, with $100 in my pocket and a bag full of dreams. The determination was larger than life: I am going to make it and it's going to be important and major! Being kept captive couldn't break me, it only made me stronger. I can handle anything, I thought!

It was more difficult than I ever thought it would be. I came here without knowing a soul, and I felt out of place and lost. I couldn't do music as I couldn't speak English very well. I went from high heels, big stages and a rock star life to cleaning people's homes just to make a few extra bucks. I had to swallow my pride, pull up my sleeves and make those dreams a realty one baby step at the time. I knew that giving up was not an option; it never was! I gave myself a year to learn enough English language so I could pursue more education and get back to teaching music. I knew that my situation was only temporary, so I believed that I could accomplish what I set out to do.

I met my husband (also a musician) and we got married in 2001. I kept going strong with my pursuit of becoming a music teacher once again. I started teaching piano and voice by traveling to people's homes. Our first son was born in 2005. As I was raising my little boy, I kept teaching and dreaming that one day I would own my own music school.

It finally happened. In 2007, we opened our first school.

I also decided to continue to further my studies in voice. Since I believe that you should always learn from the best, I made sure to get lessons from the leading vocal coach in the world - Seth Riggs. Essentially, I became certified and was given permission to teach his technique and be part of the Speech Level Singing organization.

I struggled through the years to be a teacher and a business owner. I tried to keep up with raising my kids and my duties with my family as a wife and a mother. I felt overwhelmed and always tired, not knowing what the future would bring. I started to doubt myself a lot. I also felt lonely on my journey of wanting a wonderful family and successful business, but I kept pushing forward, even though there was only one me and a hundred things to do at all times. But I did believe in making it work, tirelessly not giving up on living an American Dream in this land of opportunities. It couldn't go any other way!

I'm not crazy!

My husband and I had another son, so we had two wonderful young boys. However, our marriage had been in trouble on and off for years. Often it was a typical fight, then other times they escalated into something much more than just a typical fight.

We had ups and downs. For the last four years together, there were more downs than ups, especially when I started to get sick. In 2013, I was diagnosed with depression. Heavily medicated, I was going through countless trials of new medications. Side effects were overwhelming, leaving me at times with no recollection of what my name was, or what day it was, and feeling very estranged from my family (especially my children). I looked at them, and I knew they were my boys, yet I could not feel much. It got to be so bad that I decided to check myself into a psychiatric hospital.

I was finally properly diagnosed with bipolar one and highly functioning clinical depression. Who would ever think that the ability to fight, to make decisions, to love, to care, and to want to live could be taken by an illness? Despite the sense of defeat that I felt very often, I decided to get my life back on track and fight for survival!

As a result of my illness, our not so strong marriage started to get weaker. We pulled away from each other more and more. My escape was work; it became my addiction. I stayed away from home, and my husband and children more often. I felt less connected to him—I felt that he was blaming me for my illness by showing me his disappointment and letting me know that he "did not sign up for this". Hearing at times that I was "crazy" was taking my strength away. I started to think that I might be crazy, but as I was getting more clarity, I knew that truly wasn't the case. How I see things, how I process them, how break them apart and analyze each and every one of them, is as if I am taking tiny pieces of a puzzle and putting them all together to make a complete picture. I do this for everything. It can sometimes be a process of a few days, and it is so tiresome at times because I'm often obsessive and I won't stop until I resolve it.

I think I do understand why our way of communicating was so difficult during arguments. He sees things in black and white and I refuse; I don't know how to see things that way because I have a rainbow of colors. It's like a grey area... there is never only black and white to me. Logic is not that simple to me. Logic has so many colors, like those puzzles, and I need so many of those colorful pieces to build that big picture! My logic is simply multidimensional.

I felt so "stupid" around my husband. I constantly had to watch what I said so it didn't sound stupid, otherwise he would react negatively.

I believed less and less in our marriage. Actually, we were never friends to begin with; there was lack of understanding between us. The blame and the guilt were making me sicker. I finally came to conclusion that we were just not good for each other and I decide to leave. We wanted different things, we both strived for and believed in different principles and values.

We divorced in May of 2018.

Dear Bipolar. A personal letter to my worst enemy

My fight with bipolar and depression has been going for a few years now. It has a tremendous, ongoing impact on my relationships, the way I process information, look at life and apply myself. Writing personal notes in my journal made me understand what the illness means to me and helped me to move forward with my journey.

July 20th, 2016

"Dear Bipolar, this is a love-hate letter to you to let you know that you came to my life uninvited, unexpected, invading my mind and disrupting everything that mattered to me. You became cancer to my thoughts, and suicide to my dreams, killing them softly and quietly one after another. You are powerful and you take my strength away from me with such ease, but I keep putting up an ongoing fight. You want to get me that easy? Well, I have way too much to lose and your gain will be just another number added to your statistics. I am worth more than that..."

September 10, 2016

Thoughts, so many of them, running at the speed of light, passing through, nothing to catch them with, no wall to bounce them off. My mind is spinning from confusion. The only focus I can maintain is how upset I am, how fed up I am. Yet again, you creeped in, without warning, without invitation. I am tired physically and mentally, but I can't stop going.

My split second of clarity turns into fear... here it comes again. I am defenseless.

For someone that always tried to be in control, whether I liked it or not, that's who I was, that's who I am. Keeping that hand on a constant pulse, controlling the speed of it. Now, you robbed me of that control, and I can't feel anything else but being defeated. I hate it."

December 15th, 2016

"The first few days for me were very difficult. I didn't go to work as I was unable to keep my thoughts in check, focused and organized. Another day in battle. I start with having lots of energy, in the state of mania, feeling like I am on top of the mountain, and I can do anything. But that becomes more and more dangerous. My thoughts are racing at the speed of light. I can't see clearly anymore, as there's so much chaos and noise in my head. The noise bothers me, and I feel like I have less and less control. I know it, I feel it; and I can't do anything about it. I have to keep moving, I can't stop the motion. But then something new began happening to me. Internally it feels like I am plugged into electricity with very high voltage. I have the sensation of my mind and body being struck by lightning. At first, I enjoy the feeling. I feel like superwoman! This new sensation is strong and gives me more power. My mind keeps telling my body to GO and it responds by going faster and faster, picking up the speed that eventually gets out of control. It lasts for hours. I am in a struggle between my body in constant movement and exhaustion that's setting in, yet I am not allowed to stop. My brain doesn't accept the signals my body sends back: it's begging, I WANT TO STOP!

My rushing thoughts that are unorganized road traffic with no rules – car crashes and danger on every corner. I know who is responsible for this, but I cannot stop. I tell myself it's not my brain, it's not my vulnerability, it's YOU! Here you go uninvited again, cruelly giving me the false notion that I am in control just so you can quickly take it away! You are enjoying this! I could deal with this before because you gave me that speed and control for days before you took it away. Before, I crashed. Now, it's not only a daily occurrence but it can change from one hour to another, sometimes minute by minute. Now I am unstable, I am unreliable! I talk fast, and I can't remember thoughts or actions. I am going in circles. The worst is that I feel it. I know what is happening to me and I can't stop it. I became speed personified! Now that formerly pleasant electricity going through my body be-comes painful shock therapy. While I am in that state, the sudden crash comes in and I fall into depression. The worst part is that the speed doesn't go away. I get two in one! I can't take it anymore. I start losing the battle. My body is utterly exhausted, but my brain sends false information that I am OK and demands to keep on going. I am literally in physical pain. I start thinking, How am I going to continue to be a mom, wife, teacher and business owner? How? I can't even handle myself, so how am I going to handle the responsibility of others' lives and functionality of my surroundings? How is that going to affect my family? I know the business is starting to suffer, as a reflection of my own suffering. While healthy, I was able to pick myself up from the deepest hole and carry on with business. I never gave up. Being a teacher, I take pride in my knowledge and always strive for more so I can continuously improve. Today, it's all out of control. I keep cancelling my lessons as I am realizing that my knowledge can't just simply be put into use; it's like a large library with many, many shelves filled with books. The only problem with this picture is that none of the books are in alphabetical order. The fiction books are mixed with non-fiction, and I can't find the right book when I need it. I am exasperated. It hurts to breathe!

Now, I need lots of time to organize myself and find the 'book' that I was looking for, but during my lessons, I don't have that time. I need answers right there, right on the spot to be able to help my students. I feel helpless and fearful that my students are seeing what is happening to me... I know that I'm becoming paranoid. So, I stopped showing up. I stopped what I absolutely love to do, because of YOU, who, like a thief, took my brain function away from me."

Loving myself

The separation and divorce process was scary, unpleasant and I wanted to get it over with quickly. I've learned that no matter how strong you are, an experience like that can absolutely break your spirit, especially when I saw how much pain this brought to our young children. How could I do that? I felt so broken inside. I couldn't find the pieces of myself, as if I was missing too many of them. I had no family, no one to turn to, and my illness was taking over my life more aggressively than ever. Every day I felt like I was losing the battle. In those lowest and darkest days of my life, I saw barely any light at all. But if I tried really hard, I could see a glimpse of a tiny flicker. That tiny light was my children! I knew that if not for me, then I had to pick up the fight for them, yet again. It's my responsibility and I owed it to my children. This wasn't an overnight change; it took time. It still does. I know for certain, that one day I will thank my boys for saving my life, literally. Trying to manage my life and take charge while dealing 24/7 with an illness that affects my brain function is not an easy task. I needed to change every possible aspect of living. I needed to learn how to love my-self, yet again. I needed to figure out who am I and find myself, yet again. Who is Izabela?

I needed to figure out how to first deal with my illness while providing for my family. I had a plan; my plan was to build my music school to the point that when I am not able to teach, I can still provide for my family and not worry. It wasn't easy; not because I didn't know how to "map" my plan, but because I couldn't deliver like I could before. This time I needed to work on what seemed to be the impossible. I started to develop "codes" that would help me remember things and recall information during my classes without sitting in silence because I didn't have an answer or solution that I knew I should know.

I kept mastering my special code by placing "Alexa" in every part of my school and in every part of my house. I used "Siri" when in the car or other public places; and of course, pen and paper and my laptop became my memory. (You could say my "artificial memory".) At night, I would spend 2-3 hours just to organize everything, or to TRY to organize everything. I knew that before I could get back to business completely, I had to learn how to manage my teaching, my family and overall life, because I needed control over it desperately. I studied and started to practice Transcendental Meditation (TM) to calm my mind. I read a lot, wanting to understand the human brain, mindfulness, bipolar... anything that could help me to understand me.

I became consumed with fixing myself. I became a believer of "If you can see it in your mind, you can hold it in your hand." I saw it in my mind, but I just needed to feel it and believe it! Going from knowing, wishing and hoping, I decided to make it happen. My plan is on track, and it will take time, but I WON'T stop, I WILL SUCCEED. For the first time in my life I started to see and hear myself. I started to learn who I am as a human being. I was so glad to get to know myself.

It's my time

It's winter of a brand-new year. As I am sitting at my desk in my lovely apartment that became my home, I am excited for what's ahead of me. I'm still moving in baby steps, but I am staying my course. My future and the future of my children is much clearer now. My business is stabilizing and flourishing. My love and passion for teaching is back and I am thankful yet again to those who didn't gave up on me, my dreams and hopes. My "musical family" backed me up when I needed them the most. I am still learning about myself. Loving myself is not as easy as I thought it would be, as I am very critical and demanding of myself.

Through the years I've learned that it's easy to get knocked down to the ground, but far more difficult to pick yourself up. It takes an army to find that will. If I can give you any advice, I'd say when you are surrounded by a darkness and it seems like there is no doorway to find an exit, always look for that tiny flickering light. I promise you it's there, you just have to look much deeper and believe that you'll find it, as it's easy to miss it. We are all born warriors. Giving up is the easy part, having courage and fighting for your life are the most difficult things to put yourself through. The fear of change is what keeps us away from moving forward. Don't fear your beautiful, bright, successful future!

I truly believe if I could fight my battles and continue, you can fight them too. Although the win is not always guaranteed, the fight itself is always worth it, as it makes you stronger each and every time.

I am cheering for you! The world is cheering for you!

About the Author
Izabela Adams

Izabela Adams has been involved with the business of music education for over 25 years. She began studying voice and piano at the age of seven in her birth country, Poland.

In her twenties, Izabela was contracted to tour upscale rooms in Bahrain, UAE, as well as several European countries where she played keyboards, sang, danced, and arranged and choreographed bands for performances.

After touring, Izabela traveled to the United States where she has resided for 20 years and became a citizen. Izabela continued her music theory and performance teaching and started her own music school in 2007. That school has branched into 3 music businesses that Izabela owns & operates; The Voice Studios, The South Jersey Music Academy and Voice Productions Recording Studio in Maple Shade, NJ.

The Voice Studios is dedicated to Izabela's teaching of the Seth Riggs' Speech Level Singing (SLS) Technique. She discovered that the SLS method involved advanced techniques that helped her and her students improve their vocal skills with minimum effort. Her study of the method began in 2009, with personal training received from Seth Riggs, who has taught Stevie Wonder, Michael Jackson, Madonna, Prince, and Barbara Streisand to name a few. In 2011, Izabela became a Certified SLS instructor and the only SLS instructor in the Delaware Valley. She is also one of only 19 SLS certified instructors world-wide.

Izabela is a highly ambitious woman and when she is not teaching, she is involved with marketing her businesses and assisting her students with their careers. In 2014, Izabela joined the Music Academy Success System (MASS). In 2017, she received the "Faith-Believe-Action" Award at the Music Academy Success Conference. Through her involvement with MASS, Izabela was invited to be a guest at the Dan Kennedy MasterMind in Cleveland, Ohio in September of 2017. In 2018, Izabela was invited to join the "MasterMind for Advanced Music Academy Success" in Disney World in Orlando, Florida. Her involvement with MASS has introduced her to music industry knowledge and processes that help grow her own businesses while becoming increasingly active in her community.

Izabela is also involved in strengthening her student's futures and her community through volunteerism. She worked for 5 years with Cooper Anderson Hospital, conducting a choir for cancer survivors and prepared performances for cancer survivor events. Recently, Izabela became involved with mental health and bullying awareness non-profit organizations.

Connect With Izabela

Website: www.TheVoiceStudios.com
P: 856-779-7011
Facebook: https://www.facebook.com/TheVoiceStudios
www.SouthJerseyMusicAcademy.com
P: 856-779-7077
Facebook:
https://www.facebook.com/SouthJerseyMusicAcademy
Email: izabela_adams@me.com

Izabela Adams' Professional Credentials

- Music Teachers National Association - Member since 2007

- Maple Shade Business Association (MSBA) - Member since 2007; Advisory Board Member from 2007-2009

- Mid Atlantic Music Teachers Guild - Member since 2009; Board of Di-rectors Member from 2009-2016

- Speech Level Singing - Certified Teacher, 2011 to present

- Music Academy Success System (MASS) - Member since 2014

- The Voice Foundation - Member since 2015

- National Association of Teachers Singing (NATS) - Member since 2015

CHAPTER NINE

Strategies For Overcoming Anxiety

By Trish Scoular

Passion is derived by my innate desire to change the world. I know that sounds like I am a wannabe Florence Nightingale, but I do believe my purpose has always been helping others, which has led me on this path. I have been told *"you can't save the world"* yet my heart always yearned for something much bigger than myself, and my own adversities I have had to conquer. Even as a young girl I felt called and dreamed of traveling, cooking for many nationalities and counselling people. Growing up in a home that was considered normal and without a lot of dysfunction, I realize I was one of the lucky ones compared to others I know.

A sweet kid who was introverted, I enjoyed listening and encouraging others to live their dreams. I was also a kid who was dependent on her mother, and would walk miles after school to her work, just so I could be with her. I would show up just at closing time with our cat in my arms and near choking. When I was a toddler, my mother came home from work to find I had been missing all morning. A search had been happening, in hopes they would find me. My mother was not happy no one called her that morning, and she had come home in the early afternoon to find this news. My father was called and so were the police. Apparently, I was trying to keep up to my older brothers on their bike and got lost. When the police called later that night, they said a woman had found a toddler crying and with wet pants outside her door, which was about 10 blocks from where I lived.

At that time I didn't realize that I might be a person who suffered from anxiety even at a younger age, and someone who was incredibly sensitive to her environment. Sensitivity was in the hearts of the woman on my mother's side of the family, an aunt and a grandmother who both suffered emotional breakdowns at various times of their life. My mother was the strong one I've learned after raising 4 children while my father was away with hockey as President of the Alberta Junior, Amateur Hockey Associations and GM of the first Junior Hockey team from Edmonton. What over the years changed where I would come to be told I have generalized anxiety? A close friend I've known for years thinks I have always had anxiety after all the difficult times in my life, and what people have done to me. There were many events, all of which I cannot explain here. I was a nervous person who needed to learn that sometimes taking the high road is the best choice in moving on. I was a rather naïve girl who had a lot to learn about life, like many of us who have had to learn lessons so we could grow.

Anxiety is something that if not dealt with early on can spiral out of control, causing excessive & persistent feelings of nervousness, anxiety & fear, that can interfere with your life for an extended period of time. According to *Anxiety Disorders Association of Canada,* 1 in 4 people will have at least one anxiety disorder in their life.   In 2013, the Government of Canada reported 3 million people over the age of 18 had been diagnosed as having a mood or anxiety disorder. Generalized Anxiety Disorder is something that is persistent and at times can cause unrealistic fears about everyday life activities. Anxiety creates constant tension, pains, headaches, and leaves a person feeling self-conscious most of the time. Something called Adjustment Disorder is a brief period that creates excessive anxiety that can be an overreaction to a real-life event.

I think my own anxiety was tested when I was bullied in an RV Park. I guess that was bottom for me, while I tried to look at it as an adventure, a place to relax, and save money so I could enter the real estate world again. Who knew that going to buy a dog license would get me evicted and leave me homeless? Couch surfing, staying with friends and losing everything as a result of those circumstances. I have had to learn some hard lessons these past 25 years, but this was the biggest of them all. What appeared to be something out of the Trailer Park Boys was reality for me that year. The manager, with his ten gallon hat, loud voice and short stocky demeaner was what most in the park called *"Gestapo"*. He would drive around on his golf cart every so often, barking out orders and creating conflict with some and yet maintained friendships with others. One day I was approached by a kind woman who had been vacationing in the park for a few years with her husband, who said they had never witnessed anything quite like what was happening to me.

I was told he blamed me for everyone getting property tax notices in the mail. A property tax notice for staying long term at an RV Park? There was actually legislature in place to support people living in RV Parks who were skirted in, and were required after 6 months of permanent stay be reported to City Hall. It was a surprise for the head of BC Assessment in hearing the difficulty people were having. Apparently I was not the first of those the *Gestapo* tried to get rid of and most were women. I would hear stories of how he would remove people's trailers from the park, which was considered a criminal offense, while fighting mine. See, I made a few mistakes. The first was writing to the owners about the temperature of the hot tub, the second complaining how the roads were being unkept in that one cold winter of December and third, purchasing a dog license. I guess I stumbled naively into a situation I was unaware of and uncertain of how I would overcome. I was tired of being the target, as I had been in a work situation years prior and was told from a lawyer that character assassination was a tough case, lengthy to fight, creating only tension as a result.

This one particular Christmas Eve, when everyone was having a great time, as midnight approached, someone decided to go wake the man up. This escalated with him attacking me telling me I was acting poorly in the park and how no one liked me. Hearing that no one liked me when I thought they did, brought me back to when I was dating this man who had told me the same thing. Telling me that he could cut me up, throw me overboard and no one would care where I lived. I have to admit I laughed when he first told me that, the guy I had dated and had come back into my life after thinking I would never see him again; thankfully he's gone. Now a park manager who was treating me in a similar way, and why other than for the reasons I have explained here.

After an exchange of words and a night full of tears, I spent Christmas Day at the Homeless Shelter handing out food, with friends. I never missed my family more than at this time, or felt lonelier in my life. It was a very bad winter with 6 feet of snow and -8 degrees Celcius in temperature, very unusual for the West Coast. Living in an RV was a challenge dealing with frozen pipes, leaving the heater on when you went out so you didn't run out of propane and your dog would not freeze while you were away working. It appeared that things had calmed down and I thought the situation had blown over, as I had heard nothing since that night. It was July 13, my birthday, when a neighbor who was a truck driver asked me to go out on a run. I thought that might be fun, an experience I have never had before. Looking back, I should never have signed that release form, ending with me falling a few feet onto the concrete, wondering if I could peel my body off it and actually get up. While she stood there laughing, others gathered around to see if they could help. When I was finally upright, I could barely walk and was in a lot of pain. Going home I arrived to an eviction notice – some birthday that year! I was in tears, in a lot of pain so I asked my neighbor's husband to drive me to the emergency department for an x-ray and to get checked out.

I have never been evicted in my life and was always considered a good tenant. His friends in the park would approach me and yell from their windows, threatening to cut off my power and water (which they did), telling me it was time to go. I have never liked conflict and in the past avoided it, but something inside told me it was time to stand up. To not run from this as I had done in the past, but to face the fears in this present moment of what was happening. When we run from our fears, they only seem to follow us where ever we move to. Thoughts of "What if I pursue this eviction, what would happen as a result?" only fed my anxiety and grew with feelings of uncertainty and helplessness taking on an entire park.

Rollo May, in his book *The Meaning of Anxiety,* came up with this definition, "Anxiety is the apprehension cued off by a threat to some value, that the individual holds essential to his existence as a personality". I felt exactly what Rollo May explains, a personal attack that would affect my reputation that was good to this point.

The more I wondered why this person was attacking me, the more I realized that my path was allowing me to destroy the maladaptive patterns I have come to learn. Standing up was allowing myself a voice, despite what was happening to me, and there were others in that park who wanted to help too. This situation had set me in a place where I needed to change and grow. I would not allow myself to feel any guilt about needing to. That standing up meant going up against some prominent people in the community I was now residing in, and created even more anxiety inside, as I was thinking of starting a new business here.

At the end of this battle came no resolve, but an end to "he said, she said", allowing someone else to win against the park based on his discrimination. The journey of self continued, retreating within to discover what and why these kinds of situations kept happening. The wounds of the fall begin to creep in and the anxiety in time just worsened. It wasn't until I became friends with a man from Toronto that I realized there was some depression that had been triggered by another situation, concerning a film I was supporting. He wanted to know why I supported so many people and thought there must be something I was getting out of it. He suggested I try focusing on myself instead. I stopped and thought, you know he's right. All my life I was supporting everyone else's cause, or whatever they were doing that fulfilled them. Yes, I was an encourager and seeing others do well gave me joy, yet most of my life I knew there was more I could do, than just being that support to other people. As a result, I decided to self-publish a poetry book, published another book, founded a wellness society, developed my own affirmation cards on Loving Self, started my counseling practice and became an artist which was a life long dream of mine. I stepped outside my comfort zone and met many new people. Thankfully I had learned my lessons from the past about meeting new people and having no support moving to a new community again.

I appreciated my friend's honesty and that he held space long enough for me to share those struggles and inner turmoil. It was in this space of unraveling, then I went within and discovered that core and limiting beliefs were what had kept me from pursuing much more than I had for my life. I could have done much more than I am doing now, but lacked the self confidence and esteem to do so. It was in becoming a Counselor that I learned where I had gone wrong and how I could have lived better. Yet my path was in needing to learn the hard way, despite the struggles or the lack of tools I had. Generalized Anxiety is a disorder that can be managed and overcome. As a Counselor I see many who struggle with both depression and anxiety. It is in my ability to help treat these two disorders that I see and hear many of the same stories. Women who want to have better self-confidence, who are at times passive-aggressive because they are shy and afraid of speaking up. It is their own anxiety that is often a struggle, and depression seems to coincide. The tools we use in counseling are varied, depending on the individual. The first of what we do is a careful assessment, then a recommendation to see their family doctor as follow up if we feel they need to, and a treatment plan.

According to the World Health Organization, the aging population has seen an increase in anxiety and depression since 2005 by 14.9%. In the American Regions 7.7% are female and 3.6% are male. Mindset is difficult for someone who is struggling and not getting the help they need in discovering the root of what is causing them the anxiety and depression. It is something that can be managed if a person desires to seek the help they need and be honest about what is happening currently in their life. It's often seen in those who experience unemployment, low income populations, physical illness, trauma and life transitions.

The purpose for sharing my story is the hope that others who read it may feel inspired. To realize that they can overcome their adversities and begin to feel joy again. Most people have no purpose and it's in discovering that again, they experience a feeling of belonging. Purpose comes from doing what you enjoy, rather than focussing on that negative mindset and everything that is going wrong in your life and keeping you back from discovering purpose or achieving your dreams. Fear is what commonly keeps people from trying new approaches that would bring change and help them in the long term. The question to ask is: What is the worse that can happen by not trying something new?

Some ideas I can suggest are:

1. Make changes that reflect your behavior and activity levels. Avoiding our fears affects our confidence and just makes you feel worse. Avoidance only continues the cycle of being unhelpful and the only way to cope is by avoiding them. You may find yourself avoiding people, because you may have a different opinion and fear rejection; you may feel it's difficult to make decisions and always need someone else to decide for you. You may have a fear of talking about your feelings, or performing a task that seems difficult for you to try. This reduces your activity, keeps you feeling down and using excuses of "I'm too tired", or "I could never do that", and having negative thoughts that it will go wrong. Write a list of things you are avoiding and list some examples of activities you have stopped or cut down. Consider your pat-

terns of behavior throughout the day. What people or activities create more stress for you?

2. Track your worry. Often when we are trying to predict an outcome about something that is happening, we are often assuming the worst. It's important we evaluate the most likely and best outcome too, before responding and assuming what may not occur. Other questions to ask yourself could be:

- Are you perhaps trying to predict an outcome that may not happen?

- Are your emotions overwhelming and guiding your thoughts?

- How many times have you been wrong in the past about your worries?

- What evidence is there from your past that worrying has been useful or hurtful?

- Would you be willing to give up trying to control, if it helped you worry less?

- If you fear what happens, how would you manage the outcome?

- If your friend was worried about these same things, what would your response be to them?

- Are you basing the outcome completely on feelings or facts?

- Are you looking at the whole picture of what could be happening?

- Do you apply one set of standards to yourself and another to others?

3. Another tool we use is a Wellness Teapot. We use the teapot because it reflects how negative self talk comes from our mind, flows into our teapot and pours into our cup. We recycle those thoughts by drinking them again, which stick with us and affect how we respond to situations that occur over time. Our goal is to change our thinking by planting positive self talk instead. Until we know why negativity occurs, we cannot accept the positive ones, believing they will happen.

Some questions to ask yourself include:

- What is limiting me from believing I deserve something good?

- What negative thought is affecting my ability to believe something good will happen in my current situation?

- Is it a core belief that could be affecting and creating ongoing negativity? If that is the case, you may want to seek out counseling.

4. Establish a routine and stick to your goals. Set up a calendar that you can begin to add activities to. Start by adding a coffee with a friend or family member you have been avoiding, or going for a walk around the block. If you are in transition, ask yourself what kinds of activities you would like to start? Make a list of them and include those in your calendar. Find out when those activities start, where they meet and if there is a cost. It's hard stepping out, but know that we all have similarities we can begin conversation with; when you have this activity in common, being assertive will help overcome the worry or anxiety you may feel.

5. Exercise is important for everyone. Exercise helps people with anxiety, allowing your body to let off excessive energy that may be building. Getting out in nature can help ground and center us, as we experience the solitude while enjoying the fresh air. You could join a hiking, walking or running club. Find a personal trainer who can help you get fit and can create a safe exercise routine that works specifically for you. See a nutritionist if you are unsure about starting a weight loss program. Your family doctor is also a good resource.

6. Develop prevention skills. Know what triggers you, and have strategies in place that will guide

you when confronted with an anxious thought or worry. You can do this by journaling, and writing down how you feel; observe the thoughts you might think at that moment and how you may respond. This will help with problem solving including the who, what, why, when and how of your situation. What went through your mind at that time? How did you feel emotionally? Were you anxious, depressed or angry? What physical sensations did you feel? What did you do differently? By journaling your thoughts, you can identify patterns or themes to your worries and other areas where you may need to improve.

7. Challenge your thinking: is it helpful, unhelpful or truthful?

- Choose one thought at a time
- Clearly identify and write down what that thought is
- Avoid thoughts that start with "I am .. people are .. the world is ..." because we want to focus more on thoughts that are easier to manage.
- Label your thoughts into these three columns (helpful, unhelpful & truthful).
- Stop, think & reflect to avoid any patterns that may occur

- Experiment! Move on by acting against it! Don't be put off from what you were going to do. This thought could stop you from doing something, leading to a loss of pleasure and in the long term restrict your life by undermining your self-confidence. Make an active choice not to allow this to happen again. This requires you to live by your values and what matters most to you. Try to do the opposite of what that unhelpful thought is telling you.

- Respond with compassion to yourself! If it was your family member or friend who was troubled by unhelpful thinking, you would offer words of advice to soothe and encourage them. So give yourself the same treatment.

8. Know your values. When we know what we value, we align our goals, dreams and thoughts around them. Make a list of your values and write each one down. Apply them to your goals, dreams, friendships, and partners. For example: Trust – if we align trust with our dreams that means we need to believe they will happen, trusting in the process that everything will fall in place and that we've taken the necessary steps to achieve them. We look for trustworthy friends and partners who share these same core values.

9. Set healthy boundaries for yourself! There are many reasons why we should have boundaries. They actually help us avoid stressful situations from re-occurring by giving off red flags. Boundaries are something we all need that protect us physically, emotionally, intellectually, sexually, materially as well as our time. Often, we don't know what those limitations are because we can not say no when being asked. We are valuable and what we have to offer should be respected from ourselves and others. How many of you cross other people's boundaries? When people talk about energy vampires, they mean people who are always taking up your time. This often depletes those who are helpers, disrupting what they want to achieve in their own life. When boundaries are set, they can often disrupt a friendship or partnership if what they are getting no longer exists.

10. Learn Relaxation Techniques. There are good meditation and mindfulness apps that can help you learn how to relax. A good place to start is by putting on some soothing music that plays softly in the background, and find somewhere quiet you can sit, with no distractions. Close your eyes. When you are comfortable, begin to feel your breath. Listen as you inhale and exhale, allowing your chest to expand, never once holding your breath as your diaphragm begins to move in and out. Notice your muscles start-

ing to relax, as you begin to release any thoughts you may have, allowing your mind to relax also. Do this for about 15 minutes every day to start. There is no need to be perfect or judge, allow yourself to be free from those thoughts you may encounter.

11. Reward yourself when you achieve your first goal. Often, we neglect what we want because we are too busy stressing and worrying about money, our weight, our spouse, our children, our job or other things. When you are sticking to your new routine and finding control over your situations, you can start to reward yourself. Make a list and choose one thing that you can start doing.

12. Monitor your moods. Do you notice they alter if you are tired, feeling depressed, physically unwell, upset and worried, guilty, panicky or angry? Notice what they are and journal what is happening during each of these times and what is going through your mind at that moment, including your feelings and emotions.

13. Unplug from computers, cell phones and tablets. If we don't, we often run the risk of losing our sense of reality. It can create negative emotions, negative feelings and doubt. You may feel like you have to live up to a lifestyle that you

may not be able to achieve, by focussing on what other's might be doing. Unplugging will help with your thinking, and will keep a positive perspective on what you read. You will start to consider what is going on offline. We are losing that physical connection we all need with touch and having face to face conversations. When we allow ourselves to be controlled by our cell phones, it takes away from the intimacy we could be developing with each other.

Assertion is the key to making sure your opinions and feelings are being considered. You can be assertive without being forceful or rude. It's about knowing your feelings, rights and opinions while maintaining respect for others. It's about expressing how you feel in a direct, honest and appropriate way and knowing it's possible to stand up for yourself in a way that you don't disregard others at the same time.

In understanding assertiveness, we may need to learn the difference between passive and aggressive. Passive is always saying yes, and not allowing others to know how you feel, understand your needs, rights and not feeling safe to share your opinions. It's always choosing others' needs above your own. This is done in order to avoid conflict and to please others. Aggressive means you don't respect others, demanding things in an angry or threatening way and thinking your own needs are more important than others, ignoring their needs and thinking they have little or nothing to contribute. The aim is to win, even at the expense of others.

Remember these few points:

- Be proud of you who you are and what you do
- Understand your own needs, separate from what's expected of you
- Be clear with how you are feeling or thinking when you speak
- It's okay to make mistakes, we all do
- You are allowed to change your mind if you choose to
- Ask for time to think about it, before giving your response
- Celebrate your successes by sharing them with others
- Ask for what you want, rather than expecting others to know what you want
- You are not responsible for the behaviour of other people or for always pleasing others
- Respect others and their right to be assertive too
- Ask for clarification when needed
- Deal with others without being dependant on their approval

Changes start slowly. Don't feel like you have to do them all at once or you may feel they become unpleasant or overwhelmed keeping that cycle going. Think about how you plan to respond assertively with others, by considering the right person you need to approach. Choose the right time to approach them, know the right issue that needs addressing, and speak the right words to help them understand what it is you need. There are so many techniques that can be explored which requires a counselor to help you work through them. For those in life transitions, perhaps a coach or self help books may help. I feel that when we confront our circumstances, our thinking and the feelings that overwhelm will lessen with time. Developing strategies that work will only support our desire to do better. By using positive strategies we can learn to interact with others in a more assertive way. When we manage how we respond, we receive different results and our confidence remains strong.

In my own life, I have come to believe more in myself recently than I have in the past 40 years. I used to second guess myself by not listening to those red flags that were raised when meeting new people. I feel that if I had not learned this lesson in my life, I would still not have the confidence within to have accomplished all that I have. So many times, I shared with others my dreams and was shot down, in being told I wasn't good enough, my ideas would make no money or I wasn't pretty enough to get that man and that there were younger women I was competing with. If I had not listened to those people, I would have been farther ahead at a younger age. Even now I feel like I am living dreams I should have followed through on in my twenties but was afraid and shy, not confident in my education. My hope is that no matter what age you are reading this, that you will follow through on your desires especially if you feel called and are passionate about completing. Life is about living, loving and embracing all that is good. The bad is what we may need to learn, and if you can understand that sooner than later, you won't have to repeat the lesson again, finding you farther ahead.

About the Author
Trish Scoular

Trish Scoular is the Best Selling Author of the book "Steps to Loving You, Creating Positive Changes". She is also the author of "Whispering Thoughts: Poems About Love, Life and Living", both available on Amazon. She is a Registered Professional Counsellor who has been in practice for 4 years, and a member of the Canadian Professional Counsellor Association.

Her mission is to teach other's how to love themselves first, which isn't always an easy thing to do for many people. She also teaches how to cultivate meaningful relationships. She gives tools to help with core and limiting beliefs, defining who you are and what makes you unique, teaching boundaries, learning communication styles that work, learning positive outcomes to difficult relationships, finding your voice, building healthy relationships and learning self care/love/respect.

Her practice is seeing clients whose issues are depression, anxiety, co-dependency, addiction, trauma, abuse, low self-esteem, dealing with difficult relationships, discovering their voice, building healthy relationships, learning about self-care/love/respect, boundaries and core/limiting beliefs. She offers a workshop called Loving You, Creates Positive Change, which is for girls 12 – 17, and one for Women too.

Connect with Trish Scoular at www.trishscoular.com

She lives in Ladysmith, BC, Canada with her small dog Lily.